THE PHILOSOPHY OF THE TEACHINGS OF ISLAM

Ḥaḍrat Mirza Ghulam Ahmad

The Promised Messiah and Mahdi[as]
Founder of the Ahmadiyya Muslim Jamā'at

Translated into English by
Sir Muhammad Zafrulla Khan

Islam International Publications Ltd.

اسلامی اصول کی فلاسفی

"The Philosophy of the Teachings of Islam"
by Ḥaḍrat Mirza Ghulam Ahmad[as] of Qadian
English rendering of "*Islāmī Uṣūl Kī Philosophy*" (Urdu)
By Sir Muhammad Zafrulla Khan

First Urdu edition published in 1905, followed by several editions.

First English edition published in UK by
The London Mosque in 1979
Reprinted by Islam International Publications Ltd.
in 1989, 1992, 1996, 2007
Present revised edition (with a new format) printed in UK 2010

Published by
Islam International Publications Ltd.,
'Islamabad', Sheephatch Lane
Tilford, Surrey GU10 2AQ UK.

Printed in the UK by the MPG Books Group

Cover Design by: Salman Sajid

British Library Cataloguing in Publication data
Ahmad, Mirza Ghulam, 1835-1908
The philosophy of the teachings of Islam. 1. Ahmadiyyat
I. Title
297. 2046
ISBN 1-85372-193-X
ISBN 1-85372-198-0 Pbk

ISBN 978-1-84880-055-7

Ḥaḍrat Mirza Ghulam Ahmad Qadiani
The Promised Messiah عليه الصلاة والسلام

About the Author

Born in 1835 in Qadian (India), Ḥaḍrat Mirza Ghulam Ahmad, the Promised Messiah and Mahdi[as], remained dedicated to the study of the Holy Quran and to a life of prayer and devotion. Finding Islam the target of foul attacks from all directions, the fortunes of Muslims at a low ebb, faith yielding to doubt and religion only skin-deep, he undertook vindication and exposition of Islam. In his vast corpus of writings (including his epoch-making *Barāhīn-e-Aḥmadiyya*), his lectures, discourses, religious debates etc., he argued that Islam was a living faith and the only faith by following which man could establish contact with his Creator and enter into communion with Him. The teachings contained in the Holy Quran and the Law promulgated by Islam were designed to raise man to moral, intellectual and spiritual perfection. He announced that God had appointed him the Messiah and Mahdi as mentioned in the prophecies of the Bible, the Holy Quran and Aḥādīth. In 1889 he began to accept initiation into his Community which is now established in one hundred and ninety-eight countries. His ninety-one books are written mostly in Urdu, but some are in Arabic and Persian.

After his demise in 1908, the Promised Messiah[as] was succeeded by Ḥaḍrat Maulawī Nūr-ud-Dīn[ra],

Khalīfatul Masīḥ I. On the death of Ḥaḍrat Maulawī Nūr-ud-Dīn[ra] in 1914, Ḥaḍrat Mirza Bashīr-ud-Dīn Mahmood Ahmad[ra], who was also the Promised Messiah's[as] Promised Son, was elected as Khalīfah. Ḥaḍrat Mirza Bashīr-ud-Dīn Mahmood Ahmad[ra] remained in office for nearly fifty-two years. He died in 1965 and was succeeded by his eldest son, Ḥaḍrat Ḥāfiẓ Mirza Nasir Ahmad[rh], the Promised grandson of the Promised Messiah[as]. After seventeen years of meritorious services he passed away in 1982. He was succeeded by his younger brother, Ḥaḍrat Mirza Tahir Ahmad[rh] as Khalīfatul Masīḥ IV who, having led the Community to its present strength and global recognition, passed away on the 19th April, 2003. Ḥaḍrat Mirza Masroor Ahmad, Khalīfatul Masīḥ V[at], is the present head of the Community and enjoys the distinction of being the great-grandson of Ḥaḍrat Mirza Ghulam Ahmad[as].

Contents

Foreword to the Present Edition

The Philosophy of the Teachings of Islam is the translation of a well-known essay on Islam by Ḥaḍrat Mirza Ghulam Ahmad, the Promised Messiah and Mahdi[as], the Founder of the Ahmadiyya Muslim Jamā'at (Community). The original was written in Urdu for the Conference of Great Religions held at Lahore on December 26-29, 1896. It has since served as an introduction to Islam for seekers after the truth and religious knowledge in different parts of the world. It deals with the following five broad themes set by the moderators of the Conference:

1. The physical, moral and spiritual states of man
2. The state of man after death.
3. The object of man's life and the means to its attainment.
4. The operation of the practical ordinances of the Law in this life and the next.
5. Sources of Divine knowledge.

The essay has been published widely in many countries in numerous languages. I would like to put it on record that Ḥaḍrat Ḥāfiẓ Mirza Nasir Ahmad[rh], Khalīfatul Masīḥ III in 1978 directed me and the Late Mubarak Ahmad Saqi Ṣāḥib to compare the then existing English translation of "*The Philosophy of the Teachings of Islam*" with the original Urdu text and point out to Ḥuḍūr[rh] all the passages where the translation of the text was missing or where the translation was incorrect. By the grace of the Almighty we accomplished this task in a reasonably short time and presented it to Ḥuḍūr[rh]. At this Ḥuḍūr[rh] asked Sir Chaudhary Muhammad Zafrulla Khan[ra] Ṣāḥib to retranslate the book.[1] Sir Chaudhary Muhammad Zafrulla Khan[ra] Ṣāḥib's translation was first published in the U.K by the London Mosque in 1979 and since then it has been reprinted four times (1989–1992–1996–2007) by Islam International Publications Ltd, U.K.

The present edition has the following features:

(a) It was noticed recently that there were a few pages of the essay written by the author, which could not be included when it was published in the book form. These pages have now been included in the original Urdu edition and published, with the permission of Ḥaḍrat Mirza Masroor Ahmad, Khalīfatul Masīḥ V[at], in Rūḥānī Khazā'in Vol. 10 on pages 322, 322a, 322b, 322c and 322d. The English translation of these pages has been

1. The stock of the copies of the earlier translations was destroyed according to the instructions of Ḥuḍūr[rh].

included in the present edition of the book on page numbers 13A, 13B, 13C, 13D and 13E. The beginning and the end of these pages are marked by a star ✫.

(b) In previous editions the translation of Quranic verses in the text was literal, whereas the Promised Messiah[as] gives explanatory translation. In the present edition the Promised Messiah[as]'s translation is given in the text and the literal translation is given in the footnotes.

(c) In the earlier editions some sentences of the Urdu text were left untranslated. The translation of such sentences has been added. Moreover, at some places, the translation of some sentences was not according to the Urdu text. These have been re-translated.

(d) An index is given which was not given in the earlier editions.

For the revision and the preparation of the index etc., I was helped by Mirza Anas Ahmad Ṣāḥib, M.A, M. Litt. (Oxon), *Wakīlul Ishā'at, Taḥrīk-e-Jadīd*, for which I am extremely grateful to him.

The references from the Holy Qur'an herein cite the chapter and verse. In some renderings, the opening verse (*Bismillāhir-Raḥmānir-Raḥīm* – In the name of Allah, the Gracious, the Merciful) is not counted and readers using such editions should keep this point in mind to obtain the relevant reference that we have counted it as a verse of the Holy Quran in this book.

The name of Muhammad[sa], the Holy Prophet of Islam, has been followed by the symbol [sa], which is an abbreviation for the salutation (ﷺ) Ṣallallāhu 'Alaihi Wasallam (may peace and blessings of Allah be upon him). The names of other Prophets and Messengers are followed by the symbol [as], an abbreviation for (عَلَیْہِ السَّلَام/عَلَیْہِمُ السَّلَام) 'Alaihissalām/ 'Alaihimussalām (on whom be peace). The actual salutations have not generally been set out in full, but they should nevertheless be understood as being repeated in full in each case. The symbol [ra] is used with the name of the Companions of the Holy Prophet[sa] and those of the Promised Messiah[as]. It stands for (رَضِیَ اللّٰہُ عَنْہُ/رَضِیَ اللّٰہُ عَنْہَا/رَضِیَ اللّٰہُ عَنْہُمْ) Raḍi Allāhu 'anhu/'anhā/ 'anhum (May Allah be pleased with him/with her/with them). [rh] stands for (رَحِمَہُ اللّٰہُ تَعَالٰی) Raḥimahullāhu Ta'ālā (may Allah's blessing be on him). [at] stands for (اَیَّدَہُ اللّٰہُ تَعَالٰی) Ayyadahullāhu Ta'ālā (May Allah, the Al-Mighty help him).

In transliterating Arabic words we have followed the following system adopted by the Royal Asiatic Society.

ا at the beginning of a word, pronounced as *a*, *i*, *u* preceded by a very slight aspiration, like *h* in the English word 'honour'.

ث *th*, pronounced like th in the English word 'thing'.

ح *ḥ*, a guttural aspirate, stronger than h.

خ *kh*, pronounced like the Scotch ch in 'loch'.

ذ *dh*, pronounced like the English th in 'that'.

ص *ṣ*, strongly articulated s.

ض *ḍ*, similar to the English th in 'this'.

ط *ṭ*, strongly articulated palatal t.

ظ *ẓ*, strongly articulated z.

ع ', a strong guttural, the pronunciation of which must be learnt by the ear.

غ *gh*, a sound approached very nearly in the r '*grasseye*' in French, and in the German r. It requires the muscles of the throat to be in the 'gargling' position whilst pronouncing it.

ق *q*, a deep guttural k sound.

ء ', a sort of catch in the voice.

Short vowels are represented by:

a for ——َ—— (like *u* in 'bud');

i for ——ِ—— (like *i* in 'bid');

u for ——ُ—— (like *oo* in 'wood');

Long vowels by:

ā for ـــاـــ or آ (like *a* in 'father');

ī for ی ـــِـــ or ـــٖـــ (like *ee* in 'deep');

ū for و ـــُـــ (like *oo* in 'root');

Other:

ai for ی ـــَـــ (like *i* in 'site');

au for و ـــَـــ (resembling *ou* in 'sound').

Please note that in transliterated words the letter 'e' is to be pronounced as in 'prey' which rhymes with 'day'; however the pronunciation is flat without the element of English diphthong. If in Urdu and Persian words 'e' is lengthened a bit more it is transliterated as 'ei' to be pronounced as 'ei' in 'feign' without the element of diphthong thus 'کے' is transliterated as 'Kei'. For the nasal sound of 'n' we have used the symbol 'ń'. Thus Urdu word 'میں' is transliterated as 'meiń'.*

The consonants not included in the above list have the same phonetic value as in the principal languages of Europe.

We have not transliterated most of Arabic, Urdu and Persian words which have become part of English language, provided they are generally

* These transliterations are not included in the system of transliteration by Royal Asiatic Society.

known to English speaking people e.g., Islam, Muslim and Quran** etc.

For quotes straight commas (straight quotes) are used to differentiate them from the curved commas used in the system of transliteration, ‘ for ع, ’ for ء. Commas as punctuation marks are used according to the normal usage. Similarly for apostrophe normal usage is followed.

Munir-ud-Din Shams
Additional Wakīl-ut-Taṣnīf
October 2010

** Concise Oxford Dictionary records Quran in three forms—Quran, Qur’an and Koran.

Introduction

A person by the name of Swāmī Sādhu Shugan Chandar had spent three or four years of his life attempting to reform the Kā'isth[2] Hindu caste. In 1892 he came to the conclusion that unless people were gathered together under one roof, his efforts would be in vain. He therefore proposed to convene a religious conference, with the first one taking place in 1892 in Ajmer. In 1896, considering Lahore to be a suitable venue, he began preparations for the second such religious conference. Swāmī Ṣāḥib appointed a committee to oversee the arrangements. Master Durga Parshād was president of the committee, and Lālah Dhanpat Roy, BA, LLB, its chief secretary. The dates chosen for the convention were 26-28 December 1896, and the following six people were nominated as its moderators:

1. Roy Bahādur Bābū Partol Chand Ṣāḥib, Judge Chief Court, Punjab.
2. Khan Bahādur Sheikh Khudā Bakhsh Ṣāḥib, Judge Small Cause Court, Lahore.
3. Roy Bahādur Pandit Rādha[3] Kishan Ṣāḥib Cole, Pleader Chief Court Lahore, former governor of Jammu.

---

2. Here "th" at the end is pronounced as "th" in "three".

3. Here "dh" in the middle is pronounced as "dh" in "dharma".

4. Ḥaḍrat Maulawī Ḥakīm Noor-ud-Din Ṣāḥib[ra], Royal Physician.
5. Roy Bhawānī Dās Ṣāḥib, MA, Extra Settlement Officer, Jhelum.
6. Sardar Jawāhar Singh Ṣāḥib, Secretary Khalsa Committee, Lahore.[4]

The committee invited the learned representatives of Muslims, Christians and Aryas to set forth the excellences of their respective faiths. The objective of the Conference of Great Religions, to be held at the Lahore Town Hall, was that the excellences and the merits of the true religion be espoused in a gathering of cultured people and that its love be instilled in their hearts and that they become well acquainted with its arguments and proofs. The learned divines of every religion would thus be given the opportunity to convince others of the truth of their respective religions, while the listeners would be able to assess each speech in relation to the others and accept the truth from wherever it was to be found.

Disputes between the followers of different religions had given rise to the desire to seek the true faith. This was the best achieved by bringing together the learned preachers and teachers so that they might,

---

4. Report Conference of Great Religions. Page 253, 254 printed by Siddiqi Press, Lahore 1897.

in the context of a few published questions, set forth the beauties of their respective faiths. In such a conference, the true religion from God would definitely become patent.

This was the objective of the conference. Every learned teacher and preacher knew that he was duty-bound to make evident the verities of his faith. The conference was being held so that the truth may become manifest and it was thus a God-given opportunity for them (the learned divines) to fulfil this objective. Such opportunities were not always available to us.

Prevailing upon them further, Swāmī Ṣāḥib wrote:

"If a person sees another suffering from a fatal disease, and he firmly believes that he holds the cure for the disease, and he also claims to have sympathy for the human race, then how is it possible for him to intentionally turn away when called upon to provide a remedy? My heart is filled with the desire to know which religion is the one replete with truth. I have not the words to express my fervour."

Representatives of various religions accepted Swāmī Ṣāḥib's invitation, and the Conference of Great Religions was held during the Christmas holidays of 1896. Each of the speakers was required to address five questions published in advanced by the committee.

The committee also stipulated that, as far as possible, each speaker should confine his answers to the holy book of his religion.

The questions were:

1. The physical, moral and spiritual states of man.
2. What is the state of man after death, i.e. the hereafter?
3. What is the true purpose of man's existence on earth and how can it be achieved?
4. What are the affects of one's deeds in this life and the afterlife?
5. What are the sources of divine knowledge?

The conference was held on 26-29 December and was attended by representatives of Sanātan Dharm[5], Hinduism, Arya Samāj, Free Thinker, Brāhmo Samāj, Theosophical Society, Religion of Harmony, Christianity, Islam and Sikhism. All representatives addressed the conference, but only one of the lectures provided a true and complete answer to all five questions.

Words cannot describe the atmosphere of the conference when Maulawī Abdul Karim Sialkotī[ra],

5. Here "dh" in the beginning is pronounced as "dh" in "dharma".

most eloquently, delivered the lecture. Every person, regardless of religion, could not help but show his appreciation and approbation. There was not one person who was not engrossed and enraptured. The style of delivery was most interesting and appealing. What better proof of the lecture's excellence than the fact that even the opponents were full of praise for it. Despite being a Christian newspaper, the Civil and Military Gazette, Lahore, considered this speech to be the only one worthy of mention and it was the only one which it commended highly.

The speech was written by Mirza Ghulam Ahmad[as] of Qadian, the founder of the Ahmadiyya Muslim Jamā'at. It could not be completed in the two hours allocated for it, so the conference had to be extended for an extra day. The newspaper Punjab Observer filled column after column with applause for it. Paisa Akhbār, Chaudhwīń[6] Sadī, Ṣādiq-ul-Akhbār, Mukhbir-i-Dakkan and General-o-Gohari Āṣifi of Calcutta etc. all these newspapers were unanimous in their acclaim. Non-Muslims and non-Indians all declared the essay to be the most superior one of the conference.

---

6. Here "dh" in the middle is pronounced as "dh" in "dharma".

The secretary of the conference, Dhanpat Roy, BA, LLB, Pleader Chief Court, Punjab, wrote in his 'Report of the Conference of Great Religions':

"There was an interval of half an hour following the speech of Pandit Gordhan Dās Ṣāḥib. As the next item on the agenda was a speech presented on behalf of a renowned advocate of Islam, most people did not leave their place. The large Islamia College building began to fill up long before 1.30pm. The gathering numbered between seven and eight thousand people. Educated and knowledgeable people from various religions and nations were present and although plenty of tables, chairs and floor space had been provided, still hundreds of attendees were left with no choice but to stand. The attendees included many dignitaries, Leaders from Punjab, scholars, barristers, lawyers, professors, extra assistants and doctors. In short, different branches of educated society were all present. They stood for four to five hours listening with great patience and with rapt attention and this shows how deeply they cared for this sacred cause. The writer of the paper did not attend in person, but one of his disciples, Maulawī Abdul Karim Sialkotī, was delegated to read it at the conference. The committee had allotted two hours for the essay; however it was not finished in this time. Seeing the avid interest shown by the audience, the moderators willingly agreed to extend the session until the conclusion of the speech. This decision was in exact keeping with the wishes of the participants. Maulawī Abu Yusuf Mubarak Ali agreed to forgo his time so that Mirza Ṣāḥib's essay could be concluded. This was widely appreciated by the audience and the moderators. The conference had been due to end at 4.30 pm., but in view of the wishes of the audience it was extended to beyond 5.30 pm. The essay was delivered in four hours and from start to finish it was most interesting and well appreciated."

After receiving prophetic revelation from God, on the 21st of December 1896, a few days before the conference, the founder of the Ahmadiyya Movement publicly declared that his essay would be the most overpowering one. A translation of his declaration is presented below:

A Grand Piece of News for Seekers after Truth

[7]In the conference of Great Religions which will

7. In his announcement Swāmī Shugan Chandar Ṣāḥib has invited the leading divines of Muslims, Christians and Aryas, in the name of God, to set forth the excellences of their respective faiths in the conference proposed by him. We wish to inform Swāmī Ṣāḥib that to do honour to the name of God, as mentioned by him, we are ready to comply with his request and, if God so wills, our paper will

be held in Lahore Town Hall on the 26th, 27th and 28th of December 1896, a paper written by this humble one, dealing with the excellences and miracles of the Holy Quran, will be read out. This paper is not the result of ordinary human effort but is a sign among the signs of God, written with His special support. It sets forth the beauties and truths of the Holy Quran and establishes like the noon-day sun that the Holy Quran is in truth God's own Word and is a book revealed by the Lord of all creation. Everyone who listens to this paper from the beginning to the end, to my treatment of all the five themes prescribed for the conference, will, I am sure, develop a new faith and will perceive a new light shining within himself and will acquire a comprehensive commentary on the Holy Word of God. This paper of mine is free from human weakness, empty boasts and vain assertions.

I have been moved by sympathy for my fellow

---

be read in the proposed conference. Islam is a faith which directs a true Muslim to demonstrate perfect obedience when he is called upon to do something in the name of God. We shall now see how much regard his brothers, the Aryas and Christian divines, have for the honour of Parmeshwar or for Jesus and whether they are ready to participate in the conference which is to be held in the name of the Glorious Holy One.

human beings to make this announcement, so that they should witness the beauty of the Holy Quran and should realise how mistaken are our opponents in that they love darkness and hate light. God, the All-Knowing, has revealed to me that my paper will be declared supreme over all other papers. It is full of the light of truth, wisdom and understanding which will put to shame all other parties, provided they attend the conference and listen to it from beginning to end. They will not be able to match these qualities from their scriptures, whether they are Christians or Aryas or those of Sanātan Dharm or any others, because God Almighty has determined that the glory of His Holy Book shall be manifested on that day. I saw in a vision that out of the unseen a hand was laid on my mansion and by the touch of that hand a shining light emerged from the mansion and spread in all directions. It also illumined my hands. Thereupon someone who was standing by me proclaimed in a loud voice: *Allāhu Akbar, Kharibat Khaibar* (God is Great, Khaibar has fallen). The interpretation is that by my mansion is meant my heart on which the heavenly light of the verities of the Holy Quran is descending, and by Khaibar are meant all the perverted religions which are afflicted with paganism and falsehood, in which man has been raised to occupy the place of God, or in which divine attributes have been cast down from their perfect station. It was thus disclosed to me that the wide publication of this paper would expose the untruth of false religions and the truth of the Quran will spread progressively around the earth till it arrives at its climax. From this vision my mind moved towards the reception of revelation and I received the revelation:

"God is with you, and God stands where you stand. This is a metaphor conveying the assurances of Divine support."

I need write no more. I urge everyone to attend the conference in Lahore even at some inconvenience and listen to these verities. If they do so their reason and their faith will derive such benefit as is beyond their expectation. Peace be upon those who follow the guidance.

Ghulam Ahmad

Qadian, 21 December 1896.

It would be appropriate here to present, as a sample, the opinions of a few of the newspapers of the time:

Civil and Military Gazette, Lahore

The participants at the conference showed great interest in the lecture of Mirza Ghulam Ahmad of Qadian. His paper was an expert and flawless defence of Islam, a great number of people belonging to all sections of society came from far and wide to hear it. Mirza Ṣāḥib was unable to attend in person, so his essay was read out by a most able student of his, Maulawī Abdul Karim Sialkotī. On the 27th of December he spent three hours on the speech and it was very well received by the attentive audience. However, in the three hours he was only able to cover one of the five questions. Maulawī Abdul Karim promised that if given more time, he would continue with the lecture. The organisers and president therefore decided to extend the conference by an extra day. (Gist)

Chaudhwīń[8] Ṣadī, Rawalpindi

1 February 1897.

By far the best lecture at the conference was the one written by Mirza Ghulam Ahmad and read, in a most beautiful manner, by the renowned and eloquent speaker, Maulawī Abdul Karim Sialkotī. The lecture was delivered in a total of six hours; four

8. Here "dh" in the middle is pronounced as "dh" in "dharma".

hours on the 27th of December and two hours on the 29th, and it filled one hundred pages. The audience was captivated, every sentence met with applause. At times the audience requested that sentences be repeated over and over again. We have never before heard such a pleasing lecture. In truth, the representatives of the other religions did not address the questions posed by the conference. Most speakers dealt largely with the fourth question, only briefly passing over the other ones. A majority of the speakers talked much but said little. The exception was Mirza Ṣāḥib's paper, which gave a detailed and comprehensive answer to each of the individual questions. The audience listened with great interest and with undivided attention to a lecture which they found to be most superior and outstanding.

We are not followers of Mirza Ṣāḥib nor do we have any kind of contact with him. However we cannot be unjust in our commentary. In answering the questions, Mirza Ṣāḥib relied solely on the Quran. Every major Islamic principle was beautifully expounded using logical and convincing arguments. To first use logical arguments to prove the existence of God and to then quote the Word of God is a style which we find most charming. Not only did Mirza Ṣāḥib expound on the philosophy of Quranic teachings, he also explained the philosophy and philology of the Quranic language. In short, Mirza

Ṣāḥib's lecture was complete and comprehensive, replete with gems of knowledge, wisdom, truths and mysteries. The philosophy of the Divine was so marvellously expressed that the entire audience was left nonplussed. His lecture was the best attended with the hall being packed from top to bottom.

The entire audience listened attentively. To illustrate the difference between Mirza Ṣāḥib's lecture and those of other speakers, it would suffice to say that people flocked to hear his paper while, out of boredom, they deserted the others. Maulawī Muhammad Hussain Batalwī's lecture was poor. It was nothing but the usual banal mullahisms, there was nothing exceptional about it. Many people left during Maulawī Mauṣūf's second lecture and Maulawī Mamduḥ was not given even a few minutes extra to complete his speech. (Gist)

General-o-Gohar Āṣifi, Calcutta

24 January 1897.

(The following article was published under the dual title of 'The Conference of Great Religions' and 'The Victory of Islam').

Before discussing the conference in general, we would like to point out that (as our readers know) we have in previous editions already argued as to which learned divine presented the most powerful case on behalf of Islam. Keeping a fair and open mind, one of our distinguished correspondents elected Mirza Ghulam Ahmad of Qadian as the champion of Islam and another correspondent, in a letter to us, has expressed the same opinion. Maulawī Fakhruddin Ṣāḥib Fakhr strongly argues that Mirza Ghulam Ahmad of Qadian heads the list, followed by Sir Syed Ahmad Ṣāḥib of Aligarh. The other names he suggested as possible champions of Islam were: Maulawī Abu Saeed Muhammad Hussain Ṣāḥib Batalwī, Haji Syed Muhammad Ali Ṣāḥib Kanpuri and Maulawī Ahmad Hussain Ṣāḥib 'Aẓīmabādī. It would not be out of place to mention here that one of our correspondents also suggested the name of Maulawī Abdul Haq Ṣāḥib Delhwī, author of Tafseer-i-Ḥaqqāni. (Gist)

(After publishing an excerpt from Swāmī Shugan Chandar's invitation to the conference, the newspaper went on to say):

Having read the pamphlets publicising the conference, which of the scholars' sense of pride was awoken to champion the holy religion of Islam? How far did they take up the cause and impress upon others, by way of logical reasoning, the majesty of the Divine?

We have learnt from reliable sources that the organisers of the conference wrote letters of invitation to Mirza Ghulam Ahmad Ṣāḥib and Sir Syed Ahmad Ṣāḥib. Poor health prevented Ḥaḍrat

Mirza Ṣāḥib from attending in person, but he delegated one of his top disciples, Maulawī Abdul Karim Sialkotī, to read his paper at the conference. However Sir Syed did not attend nor did he submit a paper and it was not old-age or other commitments which prevented him from doing so. In fact he considered religious conferences to be unworthy of his attention. In responding to the invitation, (we will publish his response in one of our future editions) he wrote, 'I am not a preacher or a reformer or a Maulawī. This conference is for preachers and reformers.' Maulawī Syed Muhammad Ali Ṣāḥib Kanpuri, Maulawī Abdul Haq Ṣāḥib Delhwī, and Maulawī Ahmad Hussain Ṣāḥib 'Aẓīmabādī did not show much interest in the conference, and not one of the multitude of other learned, religious scholars of our country bothered to prepare any paper for presentation there. Admittedly, one or two people did take up the challenge, only to see their efforts rebound on themselves. As our next report will prove, they either said nothing relevant or they just made a few empty remarks. The proceedings of the conference show that it was only Ḥaḍrat Mirza Ghulam Ahmad of Qadian who truly championed the cause of Islam and that he honoured the trust people had put in himself for the representation of Islam. His representation was approved by many sects of Islam from Peshawar, Rawalpindi, Jhelum,

Shahpur, Bhera, Khushab, Sialkot, Jammoon, Wazeerabad, Lahore, Amritsar, Gurdaspur, Ludhiyana, Shimla, Dehli, Ambala, Riasat Patiala, Dera Doon, Ilahabad, Madras, Bombay, Hyderabad Dakkan and Bangalore etc... of India.

It is true to say that if Mirza Ṣāḥib's paper had not been presented, the Muslims would have been disgraced in comparison to other religions. Had it not been for the powerful hand of the Almighty, the religion of Islam would not have prevailed. It was because of Mirza Ṣāḥib's essay that Islam's glory was established. Friends and opponents alike admitted the superiority of the paper over others. In fact, once it was over even the enemies of Islam were forced to admit that the speech had helped them to understand the teachings of Islam and that Islam had been victorious. Mirza Ṣāḥib's selection as champion of Islam is most appropriate; no-one can object to his selection. He has given us reason to feel proud and in this is Islam's glory and greatness.

This was only the second Conference of Great Religions, but the size of the gathering and its high intellectual content far surpassed all other congresses and conferences. Great leaders from all the major cities of India were present and we take pride in saying that the city of Madras was also represented. The conference proved to be so interesting that instead of the advertised three days the organisers had to extend it to four days. The organisers had selected Islamia College as the venue as it was the largest public place in Lahore. But so many people participated that even this huge place proved inadequate. The great success of the conference can be seen from the fact that not only did the leading citizens of the Punjab attend, but the judges of the Chief Court and High Court of Allahabad, the honourable Bābū Partol Chand Ṣāḥib and Mr. Bannerji, were also present.

[End of the gist of Newspaper Reports]

Ḥaḍrat Mirza Ghulam Ahmad Ṣāḥib's paper was published in "*The Report of the Conference of great Religions*" Lahore and the Ahmadiyya Muslim Community has published it in book form under the title of '*Islāmī 'Uṣūl kī Philosophy*'. It has been translated into English under the title of 'The Philosophy of the Teachings of Islam '. Many editions of the book have been printed and it has been translated into French, Dutch, Spanish, Arabic, German and various other languages. Many philosophers and foreign newspapers have given it favourable reviews and many Western intellectuals have praised it highly. For example:

1. **The Bristol Times and Mirror** wrote: 'Surely the man who addresses Europe and America in this manner can be no ordinary being.' (Gist)
2. **Spiritual Journal, Boston** wrote: 'This book is good news for the whole human race.' (Gist)
3. **Theosophical Booknotes** wrote: 'This book is a most beautiful and endearing picture of Muhammad's religion.' (Gist)
4. **Indian Review** wrote: 'This book presents clear thinking and perfect wisdom and the reader is left with no choice but to praise it.' (Gist)
5. **Muslim Review** wrote: 'Anyone reading this book is bound to find a great many truths most deep and pleasing to the soul.' (Gist)

The beauty of the paper is that it does not attack any religion, it only explains the beauty and the merits of Islam. All the questions are answered with reference to the Holy Quran in a manner which proves the perfection of Islam and its superiority over all other religions.

Jalal-ud-Din Shams

ISLAM

The essay of Hadrat Mirza Ghulam Ahmad Ṣāḥib, the Chief of Qadian, which was read out by Maulana Abdul Karim Ṣāḥib Sialkotī, in Lahore in the Conference of Great Religions Dharam Mahutsu[9] on 27th December 1896.[10]

بسم الله الرحمن الرحيم
نحمده و نصلى على رسوله الكريم

It is necessary that a claim and the reasons in support of it must be set forth from a revealed book.

In this auspicious Conference the purpose of which is that those who have been invited to participate in it should expound the merits of their respective religions with reference to the questions that have been formulated. I shall today set forth the merits of Islam. Before I proceed to do so I deem it proper to announce that I have made it obligatory upon myself that whatever I state will be based upon the Holy Quran which is the Word of God Almighty. I consider it essential that everyone who follows a

9. This is Hindi expression for Great Religions.

10. This sentence is by the conveners.

book, believing it to be revealed, should base his exposition upon that book and should not so extend the scope of his advocacy of his faith as if he is compiling a new book. As it is my purpose today to establish the merits of the Holy Quran and to demonstrate its excellence, it is incumbent upon me not to state anything which is not comprehended in the Quran and to set forth everything on the basis of its verses and in accord with their meaning and that which might be inferred from them, so that those attending the Conference should encounter no difficulty in carrying out a comparison between the teachings of different religions. As all those who believe in a revealed book will also confine themselves to statements comprised in their respective revealed books, I shall not make any reference to the traditions of the Holy Prophet, inasmuch as all true traditions are only derived from the Holy Quran which is a perfect book comprehending all other books. In short this is the day of the manifestation of the glory of the Holy Quran and I humbly beseech God Almighty to assist me in this undertaking. Āmīn.

FIRST QUESTION

The Physical, Moral and Spiritual States of Man

In the first few pages of this paper I have set forth certain introductory matters which might at first sight seem irrelevant, and yet it is necessary to have a clear concept of those matters for the proper appreciation of the reply to the question that has been set out above.

Three Types of Human Actions

The first question relates to the natural and moral and spiritual states of man. The Holy Quran has indicated three separate sources of these three states. In other words, it has pointed out three springs out of which these respective states flow.

First Source: the Self That Incites to Evil

The first spring which is the source of all natural states is designated by the Holy Quran the *Nafsi Ammārah*, which means *the self that incites to evil*, as it says:

اِنَّ النَّفۡسَ لَاَمَّارَۃٌۢ بِالسُّوۡٓءِ [11]

This means that it is characteristic of the human self that it incites man to evil and is opposed to his attainment of perfection and to his moral state, and urges him towards undesirable and evil ways. Thus the propensity towards evil and intemperance is a human state which predominates over the mind of a person before he enters upon the moral state. This is man's natural state, so long as he is not guided by reason and understanding but follows his natural bent in eating, drinking, sleeping, waking, anger and provocation, like the animals. When a person is guided by reason and understanding and brings his natural state under control and regulates it in a proper manner, then these three states, as described, cease to remain the categories as natural states, but are called *moral states*.

11. the soul is surely prone to enjoin evil (The Holy Quran, Yūsuf 12:54)

Second Source; the Reproving Self

The source of the moral state of man is designated by the Holy Quran *Nafsi Lawwāmah*, as is said:

وَلَآ اُقۡسِمُ بِالنَّفۡسِ اللَّوَّامَةِ [12]

That is, I call to witness the reproving self; that is to say, I call to witness the self that reproves itself for every vice and intemperance. This reproving self is the second source of human state from which the moral state is generated. At this stage man ceases to resemble the animals. Calling it to witness is for the purpose of doing it honour, as if by advancing from the state of the self that is prone to evil and arriving at the state of the reproving self, it has become worthy of honour in divine estimation. It is so called as it reproves man on vice and is not reconciled to man's submitting to his natural desires and leading an unbridled existence like the animals. It desires that man should be in a good state and should practise good morals, and no kind of intemperance should be manifested in any aspect of human life, and natural emotions and desires should be regulated by reason. As it reproves every vicious movement, it is called the

12. And I do call to witness the self-accusing soul (The Holy Quran, al-Qiyāmah 75:3)

reproving self. Though it reproves itself in respect of vices, yet it is not fully effective in practising virtue and occasionally it is dominated by natural emotions, when it stumbles and falls. It is like a weak child who does not wish to stumble and fall but does so out of weakness, and is then remorseful over his infirmity. In short, this is the moral state of human self when it seeks to comprehend within itself high moral qualities and is disgusted with disobedience, but cannot achieve complete success.

The Third source; The Soul at Rest

The third source which should be described as the beginning of the spiritual state of man is called by the Holy Quran *Nafsi Mutma'innah*, that is to say, *the soul at rest*, as is said:

يٰۤاَيَّتُهَا النَّفۡسُ الۡمُطۡمَئِنَّةُ ۝ ارۡجِعِىۡۤ اِلٰى رَبِّكِ رَاضِيَةً مَّرۡضِيَّةً ۝
فَادۡخُلِىۡ فِىۡ عِبٰدِىۡ ۝ وَادۡخُلِىۡ جَنَّتِىۡ ۝ [13]

That is, O soul at rest that has found comfort in God return to thy Lord, thou well pleased with Him

13. And you, O soul at peace! Return to your Lord well pleased *with Him and* He well pleased *with you. So* enter you among My chosen servants, And enter you My Garden. (The Holy Quran, al-Fajr 89:28-31)

and He well pleased with thee. Now join My chosen servants and enter into My garden.

This is the stage when the soul of a person being delivered from all weaknesses is filled with spiritual powers and establishes a relationship with God Almighty without Whose support it cannot exist. As water flowing down from a height, on account of its volume and the absence of any obstruction, rushes with great force, in the same way the soul at rest flows towards God. That is indicated by the divine direction to the soul that has found comfort in God to return to its Lord. It undergoes a great transformation in this very life and is bestowed a paradise while still in this world. As this verse indicates in its direction to such a soul to return to its Lord, it is nourished by its Lord and its love of God becomes its nurture, and it drinks at this fountain of life and is thus delivered from death. This is indicated at another place in the Holy Quran where it is said:

قَدْ أَفْلَحَ مَنْ زَكّٰهَا ۞ وَقَدْ خَابَ مَنْ دَسّٰهَا ۞ [14]

That is, he who purifies his soul of earthly passions shall be saved and shall not suffer ruin, but he who is

---

14. He indeed *truly* prospers who purifies it, And he who corrupts it is ruined.(The Holy Quran, ash-Shams 91:10-11)

overcome by his earthly passions should despair of life.

In short, these three states may be called the natural, moral and spiritual states of man. As the natural urges of man become very dangerous when they are roused and often destroy the moral and spiritual qualities, they are described in God's Holy Book as the self that incites to evil. It may be asked what is the attitude of the Holy Quran towards the natural state of man, what guidance does it furnish concerning it and how does it seek to control it? The answer is that according to the Holy Quran the natural state of man has a very strong relationship with his moral and spiritual states, so much so that even a person's manner of eating and drinking affects his moral and spiritual states. If the natural state of a person is subjected to the control of the directions of divine law it becomes his moral state and deeply affects his spirituality, as is said that whatever falls into a salt mine is converted into salt. That is why the Holy Quran has laid stress on physical cleanliness and postures, and their regulation in relation to all worship and inner purity and spiritual humility. Reflection confirms that physical conditions deeply affect the soul. For instance, when our eyes are filled with tears, even if the tears are artificially induced, the heart is immediately affected and becomes sorrowful. In the same way, when we begin to laugh, even if the laughter is artificially induced, the heart begins to feel cheerful. It has also been observed that physical prostration in prayer induces humility in the soul. As a contrast when we draw ourselves up physically and strut about with our neck raised and our breast pushed forward, this attitude induces a mood of arrogance and vain glory. These instances establish clearly that physical conditions certainly affect spiritual conditions.

Experience also shows that different types of food affect the intellect and the mind in different ways. For instance, careful observation would disclose that people who refrain altogether from eating meat gradually suffer a decline of the faculty of bravery; they lose courage and thus suffer the loss of a divinely bestowed praiseworthy faculty. This is reinforced by the evidence of the divine law of nature that the herbivorous animals do not possess the same degree of courage as do carnivorous ones. The same applies to birds. Thus there is no doubt that morals are affected by food. Conversely those who are given to a diet consisting mainly of meat and eat very little of greens suffer a decline of meekness and humility. Those who adopt the middle course develop both types of moral qualities. That is why God Almighty has said in the Holy Quran:

كُلُوْا وَاشْرَبُوْا وَلَا تُسْرِفُوْا [15]

That is to say, eat meat and other foods but do not eat anything to excess, lest your moral state be adversely affected and your health might suffer.

As the soul is affected by physical conduct, in the same way sometimes the soul affects the body. For instance, when a person experiences sorrow his eyes become wet, and a person who feels happy, smiles. All our natural actions like eating, drinking, sleeping, waking, moving about, resting, bathing etc., affect our spiritual condition. Our physical structure is related intimately to our total humanity. If a certain part of the brain is injured, memory is immediately lost. An injury to another part of the brain causes loss of consciousness. Poisonous air affects the body and through it the mind, and the whole inner system, to which the moral impulses are related, is impaired and the unfortunate victim passes out quickly like a madman.

---

15. Eat and drink but do not be immoderate; (The Holy Quran, al-A‘rāf 7:32)

Thus physical injuries disclose that there is a mysterious relationship between the soul and the body which is beyond the ken of man. Reflection shows that the body is the mother of the soul. The soul does not descend from outside into the womb of a pregnant woman. It is a light that is inherent in the sperm which begins to shine forth with the development of the foetus. The Word of God Almighty conveys to us that the soul becomes manifest from the framework that is prepared in the womb from the sperm, as is said in the Holy Quran:

ثُمَّ اَنْشَاْنٰهُ خَلْقًا اٰخَرَ فَتَبٰرَكَ اللّٰهُ اَحْسَنُ الْخٰلِقِيْنَ [16]

This means that God bestows a new creation on the body that is prepared in the womb and that new creation is called the soul. Greatly blessed is God Who has no equal as a creator.

The affirmation that a new creation is manifested from the body is a mystery that reveals the reality of the soul and points to the strong relationship between the soul and the body. We are also instructed thereby that the same philosophy underlies the physical acts and words and

16. Then We develop it into a new creation. So blessed is Allāh, the Best of Creators. (The Holy Quran, al-Mo'minūn 23:15)

movements when they are manifested in the cause of God, that is to say, all these sincere actions are charged with a soul as the sperm is charged with a soul. As the framework of those actions is developed, the soul with which they are charged begins to shine and when that framework becomes complete the soul inside it shines forth in its full manifestation and discloses its spiritual aspect. At that stage those actions become fully alive. This means that when the framework of actions is completed, something shines forth from it suddenly like a flash of lightning. This is the stage concerning which God Almighty says in the Holy Quran:

فَإِذَا سَوَّيْتُهُۥ وَنَفَخْتُ فِيهِ مِن رُّوحِي فَقَعُوا لَهُۥ سَٰجِدِينَ [17]

That is, when I have completed his framework and have set right all his manifestations of glory and have breathed into him My spirit, then fall down in prostration all of you, on his account. This verse indicates that when the framework of actions is completed, a soul shines forth in it, which God attributes to Himself inasmuch as that framework is completed at the cost of worldly life. Thus the

17. 'So when I have fashioned him *in perfection* and have breathed into him of My Spirit, fall you down in submission to him.' (The Holy Quran, al-Ḥijr 15:30)

divine light which is dim in the beginning suddenly shines forth, so that on the beholding of this divine manifestation, it becomes incumbent on everyone to fall into prostration and to be drawn to that Light. Everyone perceiving that light falls into prostration and is naturally drawn to it, except Iblīs who loves darkness.

☆Here it would be useful to mention that the human foetus shows signs of life almost four months and ten days after its conception, that is, at the intermedial stage of its existence in the womb. The same laws of nature that cause the foetus to evolve from the vegetative to the animal state are also operative in spiritual birth. In other words, just as a foetus spends half the span of its existence in the privacy of the womb and then starts showing signs of animation and life, the same condition obtains in the birth of spiritual life as well.

The better part of a person's life, before the onset of senility, can be measured at approximately eighty years, half of which is forty. Here the number forty correlates with the first four months the foetus spends in the womb prior to its first physical movements. Experience tells us that when man has lived half of his productive life—the first forty years which bear a strong likeness to the first four months of a foetus' existence—his soul awakens and shows nascent signs of spiritual life, provided he is blessed with a pure disposition.

It is no secret that before he is forty a man's life is mostly obscured by ignorance. The first seven or eight years of his existence are passed in infancy, and the following twenty-five or so years are mostly spent in the pursuit of learning or frittered away on libertine pleasures. Afterwards, he is married or is otherwise beguiled into chasing wealth and honour and exceeds all bounds in doing so. At this stage, even if man turns towards God his quest is somewhat tainted with material desires. His prayers are mostly for worldly gains and his cries and supplications are sullied by worldly desires. Thus, what little faith he has in the hereafter is offset by the fact that death appears only as a distant possibility. Just as when a dam bursts its banks and destroys whatever lies in its path, so does the flood of carnal passions imperil human life. In this state, how can he ever believe in the subtleties of the hereafter? Instead, he mocks and derides religion and parades his own dry logic and sophistry. Of course, if he is good by nature, he may believe in God, but does so without full faith and sincerity and that too is conditional upon his own success. If his desires are fulfilled he turns to God, if not, he turns to Satan. In short, youth is a critical period of one's life and without Divine grace one might well land in the pit of hell. The fact is that this part of one's life is the root of all evil. It is at this time that one contracts most physical ailments and some unmentionable diseases. The mistakes made in the callowness of youth often cause man to turn away from the True and Immutable God. Thus, at this age he fears God but little and is driven by carnal passion and dominated by his baser self. He pays little heed to the advice of others and suffers the consequences of this age for the remainder of his life.

As man approaches forty, he starts shedding the vagaries of his youth and ruefully looks back at many of his follies from which his counsellors had failed to dissuade him. The ebullience of his youth naturally begins to subside, for his physical condition declines with advancing age. The rebellious blood is no longer there, nor is there any more physical vitality and recklessness of youth. The time of deterioration and decay approaches fast.

At this stage, he also witnesses the passing away of his elders and even the untimely death of younger people whose loss leaves him stricken with grief. His parents too are probably no more and the world begins to betray its transience in a number of ways. It is as if God places before him a mirror and says, 'Look, this is the reality of life of which you are so fond.' It is then that he recalls his past mistakes with regret and undergoes a radical transformation ushering in a new life, provided he is well-meaning by nature and is one of those whom God has summoned. It is in this context that Allah, the Almighty, says:

وَوَصَّيۡنَا الۡاِنۡسَانَ بِوَالِدَيۡهِ اِحۡسٰنًا ؕ حَمَلَتۡهُ اُمُّهٗ كُرۡهًا وَّ وَضَعَتۡهُ
كُرۡهًا ؕ وَحَمۡلُهٗ وَفِصٰلُهٗ ثَلٰثُوۡنَ شَهۡرًا ؕ حَتّٰۤى اِذَا بَلَغَ اَشُدَّهٗ وَ بَلَغَ
اَرۡبَعِيۡنَ سَنَةً ۙ قَالَ رَبِّ اَوۡزِعۡنِىۡۤ اَنۡ اَشۡكُرَ نِعۡمَتَكَ الَّتِىۡۤ اَنۡعَمۡتَ
عَلَىَّ وَعَلٰى وَالِدَىَّ وَاَنۡ اَعۡمَلَ صَالِحًا تَرۡضٰٮهُ وَاَصۡلِحۡ لِىۡ فِىۡ ذُرِّيَّتِىۡ ۚ
اِنِّىۡ تُبۡتُ اِلَيۡكَ وَاِنِّىۡ مِنَ الۡمُسۡلِمِيۡنَ ۝ [18]

That is, we enjoined on man [saying to him:] "Be good to your parents. You should realize what agony your mother suffered for you! During your pregnancy she suffered pain for a long period of time and with pain she brought you forth. For thirty months she remained in discomfort during gestation and breast-feeding you. Again, He says that when a good person reaches forty and matures he recalls Divine exhortations and says, 'My Lord, let me be grateful for the favours You have bestowed on me and on my parents and grant me the opportunity to do such good

---

18. And We have enjoined on man to be good to his parents. His mother bears him with pain, and brings him forth with pain. And the bearing of him and his weaning takes thirty months, till, when he attains his full maturity and reaches *the age of* forty years, he says, 'My Lord, grant me *the power* that I may be grateful for Your favour which You have bestowed upon me and upon my parents, and that I may do such good works as may please You. And make my seed righteous for me. I do turn to You; and, truly, I am of those who submit *to You*.' (The Holy Quran, al-Aḥqāf 46:16)

works as may please You, and make my seed righteous for me. That is to say, if I failed in my duty to my parents, let not my children do the same. If ever I strayed from the right path, let them not follow suit. My Lord, I repent and turn to You and am of those who submit.'

Thus, God has made it clear that the fortieth year is a blessing for those who are righteous and it is then that the spirit of truth awakens in them. Most of God's Prophets were raised in the fortieth year of their lives. For instance, our Lord and Master, the Holy Prophet[sa] was also raised for the reformation of mankind in his fortieth year. ☆

The soul is created

After this digression I revert to my earlier discussion. It is absolutely true that the soul is a fine light developed inside the body and which is nurtured in the womb. To begin with it is hidden and imperceptible and later it is made manifest. From the very beginning its essence is present in the sperm. It is related to the sperm in a mysterious manner by the design and command and will of God. It is a bright and illumined quality of the sperm. It cannot be said that it is a part of the sperm as matter is part of matter, nor can it be said that it comes from outside or falls upon the earth and gets mixed with the matter of the sperm. It is latent in the sperm as fire is latent in the flint. The Book of God does not mean that the soul descends from heaven as a separate entity or falls upon the earth from the atmosphere and then by chance gets mixed with the sperm and enters the womb with it. There is no basis for such a notion. The law of nature rejects it. We observe daily that thousands of insects infect impure and stale foods and are generated in unwashed wounds. Dirty linen secretes hundreds of lice and all sorts of worms are generated inside a person's stomach. It cannot be said that all these come from outside or can be observed as descending from heaven. The truth is that the soul is developed in the body and this also proves that it is created and is not self-existent.

The second birth of the Soul

Now what I mean to emphasise here is that the design of the Almighty Who has created the soul from the body with His perfect power appears to be that the second birth of the soul should also take place through the body. The movements of the soul follow the movements of the body. If the body is drawn in a particular direction the soul automatically follows it. It is, therefore, a function of the Book of God to direct itself to the natural state of man: that is why the Holy Quran pays so much attention to the reform of the natural state of man and gives directions with regard to everyone of his actions, his laughing, weeping, eating, clothing, sleeping, speaking, keeping silent, marrying, remaining celibate, walking, standing still, outward cleanliness, bathing, submitting to a discipline in health and in illness etc. It affirms that man's physical condition affects his spiritual condition deeply. I cannot undertake a detailed exposition of all those directions as time is not available for such an undertaking.

Gradual Progress of Man

When I reflect upon the Holy Word of God, it becomes clear to me how He bestows on man, through His teachings, rules for the reform of his natural condition and then gradually lifts him upwards and desires to raise him to the highest spiritual state, I realize that the principle of profound spiritual insight [underlying the following Divine Scheme] is that first God desires to teach man the rules of social behaviour like sitting, standing, eating, drinking, talking etc., and thus to deliver him from a state of barbarism and distinguish him from the animals and thus bestow upon him an elementary moral state which might be described as social culture. He then desires to regulate his elementary moral habits so that they should acquire the character of high moral qualities. Both these methods are part of the same process as they are related to the reform of man's natural condition. There is between them a difference only of degree. The All-Wise One has so arranged the moral system that man should be able to rise from a low to a high moral condition.

The true meaning of Islam

The third grade of progress is that a person should become wholly devoted to the love of his True Creator and to the winning of His pleasure. The whole of his being should be committed to God. To remind Muslims constantly of this grade their religion has been named Islam, which means to devote oneself wholly to God and to keep nothing back. As God, the Glorious, has said:

بَلٰى ۚ مَنْ اَسْلَمَ وَجْهَهٗ لِلّٰهِ وَهُوَ مُحْسِنٌ فَلَهٗۤ اَجْرُهٗ عِنْدَ رَبِّهٖ ۪
وَلَا خَوْفٌ عَلَيْهِمْ وَلَا هُمْ يَحْزَنُوْنَ ۝ [19]

قُلْ اِنَّ صَلَاتِيْ وَنُسُكِيْ وَمَحْيَايَ وَمَمَاتِيْ لِلّٰهِ رَبِّ الْعٰلَمِيْنَ ۝
لَا شَرِيْكَ لَهٗ ۚ وَبِذٰلِكَ اُمِرْتُ وَاَنَا اَوَّلُ الْمُسْلِمِيْنَ ۝ [20]

وَاَنَّ هٰذَا صِرَاطِيْ مُسْتَقِيْمًا فَاتَّبِعُوْهُ ۚ وَلَا تَتَّبِعُوا السُّبُلَ فَتَفَرَّقَ بِكُمْ
عَنْ سَبِيْلِهٖ ۭ [21]

---

19. Nay, whoever submits himself completely to Allāh, and is the doer of good, shall have his reward with his Lord. No fear *shall come* upon such, neither shall they grieve. (The Holy Quran, al-Baqarah 2:113)

20. Say, 'My Prayer and my sacrifice and my life and my death are *all* for Allāh, the Lord of the worlds. 'He has no partner. And so am I commanded, and I am the first of those who submit.' (The Holy Quran, al-An'ām 6:163-164)

21. 'This is My path *leading* straight. So follow it; and follow not *other* ways, lest they lead you away from His way. (The Holy Quran, al-An'ām 6: 154)

قُلْ إِنْ كُنْتُمْ تُحِبُّونَ اللّٰهَ فَاتَّبِعُوْنِيْ يُحْبِبْكُمُ اللّٰهُ وَيَغْفِرْ لَكُمْ
ذُنُوْبَكُمْ ۗ وَاللّٰهُ غَفُوْرٌ رَّحِيْمٌ ○ [22]

Salvation means that a person should commit himself wholly to God, and should offer himself as a sacrifice in the cause of God, and should prove his sincerity not only through his motive but also through righteous conduct. He who so comports himself will have his recompense from God. Such people shall have no fear nor shall they grieve.

Tell them: My prayer and my sacrifices, my living and my dying are all for the sake of God, Whose providence comprehends everything and Who has no associate. So have I been commanded and I am the foremost of those who fulfil this concept of Islam and offer themselves as a sacrifice in the cause of Allah.

This is My straight path then follow it and do not follow any other path which will lead you away from His path.

Tell them: If you love God then follow me and walk along my path so that God may love you and forgive you your sins. He is Most Forgiving Ever Merciful.

---

22. Say, 'If you love Allāh, follow me: *then* will Allāh love you and forgive you your faults. And Allāh is Most Forgiving, Merciful.' (The Holy Quran, āl-e-'Imrān 3:32)

Distinction Between the Natural and Moral States

I shall now proceed to describe the three states of man. But before I do so, it is necessary for me to voice a reminder that, as indicated in the Holy Word of God Almighty, the natural state of man, the fountainhead of which is the self that incites to evil, is not something divorced from his moral state. The Holy Word of God has classified man's natural faculties and desires and urges, as natural conditions. These, when they are consciously regulated and controlled and are brought into action on their proper occasions and places, become moral qualities. In the same way, moral conditions are not entirely distinct from spiritual conditions. When moral conditions develop absolute devotion to God and complete purification of self and, cutting asunder from the world, turn wholly to God and to perfect love and complete devotion and full serenity and satisfaction and complete accord with the Divine will, they become spiritual conditions.

So long as his natural conditions are not converted into moral conditions, man deserves no praise, inasmuch as they are to be found in other animates and even in solids also. In the same way the mere acquisition of moral qualities does not bestow spiritual life upon a person. A person who denies the existence of God can yet exhibit good moral qualities, such as to be humble of heart, to seek peace, to discard evil and not to resist the evil-monger. These are all natural conditions which may be possessed even by an unworthy one who is utterly unacquainted with the fountainhead of salvation and enjoys no part of it. Many animals have a gentle disposition, and can be trained to become wholly peaceful and not to react savagely to chastisement, and yet we cannot call them human, let alone humans of high status. In the same way, a person who is entirely misguided and even suffers from some vices, can exhibit these qualities.

The refutation of the Doctrine of Preservation of Life

It is possible that a person may develop mercy to a degree in which he would not permit himself to kill the germs that might be generated in his wounds, or might be so mindful of preserving life that he may not wish to harm the lice in his hair or the insects that are generated in his stomach and his arteries and his brain. I can believe that a person's mercy might impel him to discard the use of honey as it is procured by the destruction of many lives and by driving the poor bees out of their hives. I can believe that a person may avoid the use of musk as it is the blood of a poor animal and is procured by slaughtering it and separating it from its young. I do not deny that a person might refrain from wearing pearls or silk as both these are procured through the death of worms. I can even understand that a person in pain might refuse to be bled by leeches and might prefer to suffer pain himself rather than desire the death of poor leeches. I can even believe that a person might carry his mercy and regard for life to a degree that he might refuse to drink water in order to spare the germs in the water. I can accept all this, but I cannot accept that these natural conditions can be regarded as moral qualities or that they can serve to wash out the inner impurities which obstruct a person's approach to God. I cannot believe that to become harmless to a degree in which some animals and birds excel man can become the means of the acquisition of a high degree of humanity. Indeed, I consider this attitude as amounting to opposition to the law of nature and inconsistent with the high moral quality of seeking the pleasure of God. It rejects the bounties that nature has bestowed upon us. Spirituality can be achieved only through the use of every moral quality in its proper place and on its proper occasion, and through treading faithfully upon the ways of God and through being wholly devoted to Him. He who becomes truly God's cannot exist without Him. A true seeker after God is like a fish sacrificed by the hand of God and its water is the love of God.

Three Methods of Reform

After this digression I revert to my earlier discussion. I have just mentioned that there are three springs from which human states flow, namely, the self that incites to evil, the self that reproves and the soul at rest. There are also three methods of reform. The first is that senseless savages should be taught the elementary social values pertaining to eating, drinking, marriage etc. They should not go about naked nor eat carrion, like dogs, nor practise any other type of wildness. This is an elementary stage of the reform of natural conditions of the type that would have to be adopted, for instance, if it is desired to teach a savage from Port Blair, the elementary ways of human behaviour.

The second method of reform is that when a person has adopted elementary human ways, he may be taught the higher moral qualities and should be instructed to employ his faculties in their proper places and on their proper occasions.

The third method of reform is that those who have acquired high moral qualities should be given a taste of the draught of the love of and union with God. These are Methods which Nobel Quran has mentioned.

The Advent of the Holy Prophet at the Time of the Greatest Need

Our lord and master, the Holy Prophet, peace and blessings of Allah be upon him, was raised at a time when the world had been thoroughly corrupted. As God Almighty has said:

ظَهَرَ الْفَسَادُ فِي الْبَرِّ وَالْبَحْرِ [23]

Corruption has spread over land and sea. This means that the People of the Book, as well as those who had no experience of revelation, had all been corrupted. The purpose of the Holy Quran was to revive the dead, as is said:

اِعْلَمُوْٓا اَنَّ اللّٰهَ يُحْيِ الْاَرْضَ بَعْدَ مَوْتِهَا [24]

Know that Allah is about to revive the earth after its death.

---

23. Corruption has appeared on land and sea (The Holy Quran, ar-Rūm 30:42)

24. Know that Allāh is *now* quickening the earth after its death. (The Holy Quran, al-Ḥadīd 57:18)

At that time the people of Arabia were steeped in barbarism. No social pattern prevailed and they took pride in every type of sin and misconduct. A man married an unlimited number of wives, and they were all addicted to the use of everything unlawful. They considered it lawful to marry their mothers, and that is why God Almighty had to prescribe:

حُرِّمَتْ عَلَيْكُمْ اُمَّهٰتُكُمْ [25]

That is, today your mothers are made unlawful for you. They ate carrion and some of them were even cannibals. There is not a sin of which they were not guilty. Most of them did not believe in the after life. Many of them denied the existence of God. They killed their female infants with their own hands. They killed orphans and devoured their substance. They had the appearance of human beings but were bereft of reason. They possessed no modesty, no shame, and no self respect. They drank liquor like water. The one among them who indulged indiscriminately in fornication was acknowledged as the chief of his tribe. They were so utterly ignorant that their neighbouring people called them the unlettered ones. At such time and for the reform of such people, our lord and master, the Holy Prophet, peace and

25. Forbidden to you are your mothers, (The Holy Quran, an-Nisā' 4:24)

blessings of Allah be upon him, appeared in Mecca. This was the time that called for the three types of reform that we have just mentioned. That is why the Holy Quran claims to be more complete and more perfect than all other books of guidance, inasmuch as the other books had not the opportunity of carrying out the three types of reforms which the Holy Quran was designed to carry out. The purpose of the Holy Quran was to elevate savages into men, and then to equip them with moral qualities, and finally raise them to the level of godly persons. The Holy Quran thus comprehends all those three projects.

The True Purpose of the Teachings of the Holy Quran is the Reform of the Three Conditions:

Before I embark upon a detailed exposition of the threefold reforms that I have just mentioned, it is necessary to point out that there is no teaching in the Holy Quran which is imposed by compulsion. The whole purpose of the Quran is the three reforms, and all its teachings are directed towards that end. All other directions are the means for the achievement of those reforms. As sometimes a surgeon has to perform an operation in order to restore the patient to normal health, or has to apply an ointment, in the same way the teachings of the Quran, out of sympathy for mankind, have recourse to such means also. The purpose of all Quranic insights and admonitions and directions is to raise man from his natural condition of barbarity to a moral state, and then to lift him from that state to the limitless ocean of spirituality.

Natural Conditions by Regulation become Moral Qualities

We have already stated that natural conditions are not something distinct from moral conditions. When they are regulated and are used on their proper occasions, under the direction of reason, they acquire a moral character. Before they are controlled by reason and understanding they have not the character of moral qualities, but are natural impulses, however much they might resemble moral qualities. For instance, if a dog or lamb displays affection or docility towards its master it would not be described as moral or good-mannered. In the same way a wolf or a tiger would not be described as ill-mannered on account of its wildness. A moral state emerges after reflection and regard for time and occasion come into play. A person who does not exercise reason and deliberation is like a child whose mind and intellect are not yet governed by reason, or is like a madman who has lost his reason and good sense. A child or a mad man sometimes behaves in a manner that has the appearance of moral action, but no sensible person calls such conduct moral, as such conduct does not proceed from good sense and appropriateness, but is a natural reaction to the circumstances. A human infant, as soon as it is born, seeks its mother's breasts, and a chicken, as soon as it is hatched begins to pick up corn. In the same way the spawn of a leech behave like a leech, a baby serpent behaves like a serpent and a tiger cub behaves like a tiger. A human infant begins to exhibit human reactions as soon as it is born and those reactions become more and more remarkable as it begins to grow up. For instance, its weeping becomes louder, and its smiles become laughter, and its gaze becomes more concentrated. At the age of a year or eighteen months it develops another natural trait: it begins to display its pleasure and displeasure through its movements and tries to strike someone or to give something to someone. All these motions are natural impulses. Similarly a barbarian who possesses little human sense is like such an infant and displays natural impulses in his words, actions and movements and is governed by his natural emotions. Nothing proceeds from him in consequence of the exercise of his inner faculties. Whatever surges up from his inside under the operation of a natural impulse and as a reaction to external stimuli, becomes manifest. It is possible that his natural impulses that are exhibited as a reaction to an external stimulus may not all be vicious, and some might resemble good morals, but they are normally not the consequences of reasonable reflection and consideration, and even if they are to some degree so motivated they cannot be relied upon on account of the domination of natural impulses.

True Morals

In short we cannot attribute true morals to a person who is subject to natural impulses like animals or infants or the insane, and who lives more or less like animals. The time of true morals, whether good or bad, begins when a person's reason becomes mature and he is able to distinguish between good and bad and the degree of evil and goodness, and begins to feel sorry when he misses an opportunity of doing good and is remorseful when he has done some wrong. This is the second stage of his life which is designated by the Holy Quran the self that reproves. It should, however be remembered that casual admonition is not enough to lead a barbarian to the stage of the self that reproves. It is necessary that he should become conscious of the existence of God to a degree at which he should not consider his creation as without purpose, so that an understanding of the Divine should stimulate his true moral qualities. That is why God Almighty has drawn attention to the need of understanding of the Divine, and has assured man that every act and moral produces an effect which brings about spiritual comfort or spiritual pain in this life, and will be manifested clearly in the hereafter. In short, at the stage of the self that reproves, a person is bestowed so much of reason and understanding and good conscience, that he reproves himself over a wrong done by him and is anxious to do good. That is the stage when a person acquires high moral qualities.

Distinction Between *Khalq* (creation) and *Khulq* (morals)

Here I would like to define the word "*Khulq*". It should be kept in mind that "*Kh*" in the word "*Khalq*" followed by *Fatḥa*[26] denotes physical birth, and "*Kh*" in the word "*Khulq*" followed by *Zamma*[27] denotes the spiritual birth. *Khalq* connotes physical birth and *Khulq* connotes inner birth. As inner birth is perfected

26. It is a vowel-sound equal to short "a"– as "a" in human.

27. It is a vowel-sound equal to short "u"– as "u" in put.

through moral development and not merely through the exercise of natural impulses, *Khulq* connotes moral qualities and not natural impulses. It should be pointed out that the common conception that morals merely mean meekness, courtesy and humility is entirely mistaken. The truth is that corresponding to every physical action there is an inner quality which is moral; for instance, a person sheds tears through the eyes and corresponding to that action there is an inner quality which is called tenderness, which takes on the character of a moral quality when, under the control of reason, it is exercised on its proper occasion. In the same way, a person defends himself against the attack of an enemy with his hands, and corresponding to this action there is an inner quality which is called bravery. When this quality is exercised at its proper place and on its proper occasion, it is called a moral quality. Similarly a person sometimes seeks to relieve the oppressed from the oppression of tyrants, or desires to make provision for the indigent and the hungry, or wishes to serve his fellow beings in some other way, and corresponding to such action there is an inner quality which is designated mercy. Sometimes a person punishes a wrongdoer and corresponding to such action there is an inner quality which is called retribution. Sometimes a person does not wish to attack one who attacks him and forbears to take action against a wrongdoer, corresponding to which there is a quality which is called forbearance or endurance. Sometimes a person works with his hands or feet or employs his mind and intellect or his wealth in order to promote the welfare of his fellow beings, corresponding to which there is an inner quality which is called benevolence. Thus, when a person exercises all these qualities on their proper occasions and at their proper places they are called moral qualities. God, the Glorious, has addressed the Holy Prophet, peace and blessings of Allah be upon him, in the words:

اِنَّكَ لَعَلٰى خُلُقٍ عَظِيْمٍ [28]

That is, thou dost most surely possess high moral excellences. This means that all high moral qualities such as benevolence, courage, justice, mercy, bountifulness, sincerity, high mindedness etc. were combined in the person of the Holy Prophet. In short all the natural qualities of man as courtesy, modesty, integrity, benevolence, jealousy, steadfastness, chastity, piety, equity, sympathy, bravery, generosity, forbearance, endurance,

---

28. And you do surely possess high moral excellences. (The Holy Quran, al-Qalam 68:5)

bountifulness, sincerity, loyalty etc., when they are manifested on their proper occasions under the guidance of reason and reflection would all be accounted moral qualities. In reality they are the natural states and impulses of man and are designated moral qualities when they are exercised deliberately on their proper occasions. A natural characteristic of man is that he desires to make progress and, therefore, through following a true religion and keeping good company and conforming to good teachings he converts his natural impulses into moral qualities. No other animal is invested with this characteristic.

Natural States of Man

We shall now proceed to set forth the first of the three reforms which is inculcated by the Holy Quran and which is related to the natural state of man. This reform relates to what are known as good manners, that is to say, the code that regulates the natural conditions of barbarians, like eating, drinking, marriage, etc., and establishes them at a just level of social values and rescues them from an animal existence. In this context the Holy Quran ordains:

حُرِّمَتْ عَلَيْكُمْ اُمَّهٰتُكُمْ وَبَنٰتُكُمْ وَاَخَوٰتُكُمْ وَعَمّٰتُكُمْ وَخٰلٰتُكُمْ
وَبَنٰتُ الْاَخِ وَبَنٰتُ الْاُخْتِ وَاُمَّهٰتُكُمُ الّٰتِيْٓ اَرْضَعْنَكُمْ وَاَخَوٰتُكُمْ
مِّنَ الرَّضَاعَةِ وَاُمَّهٰتُ نِسَآئِكُمْ وَرَبَآئِبُكُمُ الّٰتِيْ فِيْ حُجُوْرِكُمْ مِّنْ
نِّسَآئِكُمُ الّٰتِيْ دَخَلْتُمْ بِهِنَّ فَاِنْ لَّمْ تَكُوْنُوْا دَخَلْتُمْ بِهِنَّ فَلَا جُنَاحَ عَلَيْكُمْ
وَحَلَآئِلُ اَبْنَآئِكُمُ الَّذِيْنَ مِنْ اَصْلَابِكُمْ وَاَنْ تَجْمَعُوْا بَيْنَ الْاُخْتَيْنِ اِلَّا
مَا قَدْ سَلَفَ 29

لَا يَحِلُّ لَكُمْ اَنْ تَرِثُوا النِّسَآءَ كَرْهًا 30

وَلَا تَنْكِحُوْا مَا نَكَحَ اٰبَآؤُكُمْ مِّنَ النِّسَآءِ اِلَّا مَا قَدْ سَلَفَ 31

اُحِلَّ لَكُمُ الطَّيِّبٰتُ ...... وَالْمُحْصَنٰتُ مِنَ الْمُؤْمِنٰتِ وَالْمُحْصَنٰتُ مِنَ
الَّذِيْنَ اُوْتُوا الْكِتٰبَ مِنْ قَبْلِكُمْ اِذَآ اٰتَيْتُمُوْهُنَّ اُجُوْرَهُنَّ
مُحْصِنِيْنَ غَيْرَ مُسٰفِحِيْنَ وَلَا مُتَّخِذِيْٓ اَخْدَانٍ 32

---

29. Forbidden to you are your mothers, and your daughters, and your sisters, and your fathers' sisters, and your mothers' sisters, and brother's daughters, and sister's daughters, and your *foster*-mothers that have given you suck, and your foster-sisters, and the mothers of your wives, and your step-daughters, who are your wards by your wives unto whom you have gone in—but if you have not gone in unto them, there shall be no sin upon you—and the wives of your sons that are from your loins; and *it is forbidden* to you to have two sisters together in marriage, except what has already passed; (The Holy Quran, an-Nisā' 4:24)

30. It is not lawful for you to inherit women against their will; (The Holy Quran, an-Nisā' 4:20)

31. And marry not those women whom your fathers married, except what has already passed. (The Holy Quran, an-Nisā' 4:23)

32. Good things have been made lawful for you ... And *lawful for you are* chaste believing women and chaste women from among those who were given the Book before you, when you give them their dowries,

وَلَا تَقْتُلُوٓا اَنْفُسَكُمْ 33

وَلَا تَقْتُلُوٓا اَوْلَادَكُمْ 34

لَا تَدْخُلُوْا بُيُوْتًا غَيْرَ بُيُوْتِكُمْ حَتّٰى تَسْتَاْنِسُوْا وَتُسَلِّمُوْا عَلٰٓى اَهْلِهَا 35
فَاِنْ لَّمْ تَجِدُوْا فِيْهَآ اَحَدًا فَلَا تَدْخُلُوْهَا حَتّٰى يُؤْذَنَ لَكُمْ ۚ وَاِنْ
قِيْلَ لَكُمُ ارْجِعُوْا فَارْجِعُوْا هُوَ اَزْكٰى لَكُمْ 36

وَاْتُوا الْبُيُوْتَ مِنْ اَبْوَابِهَا 37

وَاِذَا حُيِّيْتُمْ بِتَحِيَّةٍ فَحَيُّوْا بِاَحْسَنَ مِنْهَآ اَوْ رُدُّوْهَا 38

اِنَّمَا الْخَمْرُ وَالْمَيْسِرُ وَالْاَنْصَابُ وَالْاَزْلَامُ رِجْسٌ مِّنْ
عَمَلِ الشَّيْطٰنِ فَاجْتَنِبُوْهُ لَعَلَّكُمْ تُفْلِحُوْنَ 39

---

contracting valid marriage and not committing fornication nor taking secret paramours. (The Holy Quran, al-Mā'idah 5:6)

33. And kill not yourselves. (The Holy Quran, an-Nisā' 4:30)

34. And that you kill not your children (The Holy Quran, al-An'ām 6:152)

35. Enter not houses other than your own until you have asked leave and saluted the inmates thereof. (The Holy Quran, an-Nūr 24:28)

36. And if you find no one therein, do not enter them until you are given permission. And if it be said to you, 'Go back' then go back; that is purer for you. (The Holy Quran, an-Nūr 24:29)

37. And you should come into houses by the doors thereof; (The Holy Quran, al-Baqarah 2:190)

38. And when you are greeted with a prayer, greet you with a better prayer or *at least* return it. (The Holy Quran, an-Nisā' 4:87)

39. Wine and the game of hazard and idols and divining arrows are only an abomination of Satan's handiwork. So shun *each one* of them that you may prosper. (The Holy Quran, al-Mā'idah 5:91)

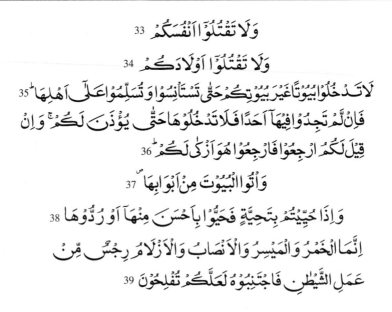

حُرِّمَتْ عَلَيْكُمُ الْمَيْتَةُ وَالدَّمُ وَلَحْمُ الْخِنْزِيرِ وَمَآ أُهِلَّ لِغَيْرِ اللّٰهِ

بِهٖ وَالْمُنْخَنِقَةُ وَالْمَوْقُوذَةُ وَالْمُتَرَدِّيَةُ وَالنَّطِيحَةُ وَمَآ أَكَلَ السَّبُعُ

اِلَّامَا ذَكَّيْتُمْ وَمَا ذُبِحَ عَلَى النُّصُبِ ﴿40﴾

يَسْئَلُوْنَكَ مَاذَآ أُحِلَّ لَهُمْ قُلْ أُحِلَّ لَكُمُ الطَّيِّبٰتُ ﴿41﴾

اِذَاقِيْلَ لَكُمْ تَفَسَّحُوْا فِى الْمَجٰلِسِ فَافْسَحُوْا يَفْسَحِ اللّٰهُ لَكُمْ وَاِذَا

قِيْلَ انْشُزُوْا فَانْشُزُوْا ﴿42﴾

كُلُوْا وَاشْرَبُوْا وَلَا تُسْرِفُوْا ﴿43﴾

وَقُوْلُوْا قَوْلًا سَدِيْدًا ﴿44﴾

وَثِيَابَكَ فَطَهِّرْ وَالرُّجْزَ فَاهْجُرْ ﴿45﴾

وَاقْصِدْ فِىْ مَشْيِكَ وَاغْضُضْ مِنْ صَوْتِكَ ﴿46﴾

---

40. Forbidden to you is *the flesh of an animal* which dies of itself, and blood and the flesh of swine; and that on which is invoked the name of one other than Allāh; and that which has been strangled; and that beaten to death; and that killed by a fall; and that which has been gored to death; and that of which a wild animal has eaten, except that which you have properly slaughtered; and that which has been slaughtered at an altar. (The Holy Quran, al-Māʾidah 5:4)

41. They ask you what is made lawful for them. Say, 'All good things have been made lawful for you; (The Holy Quran, al-Māʾidah 5:5)

42. When it is said to you, 'Make room!' in *your* assemblies, then do make room; Allāh will make ample room for you. And when it is said, 'Rise up!' then rise up; (The Holy Quran, al-Mujādalah 58:12)

43. Eat and drink but exceed not the bounds; (The Holy Quran, al-Aʿrāf 7:32)

44. And say the right word. (The Holy Quran, al-Ahzāb 33:71)

45. And your heart do you purify, And uncleanliness do you shun, (The Holy Quran, al-Muddaththir 74:5-6)

46. 'And walk you at a moderate pace, and lower your voice; (The Holy Quran, Luqmān 31:20)

تَزَوَّدُوا فَإِنَّ خَيْرَ الزَّادِ التَّقْوٰى 47

وَإِنْ كُنْتُمْ جُنُبًا فَاطَّهَّرُوا 48

وَفِيْٓ أَمْوَالِهِمْ حَقٌّ لِّلسَّآئِلِ وَالْمَحْرُوْمِ 49

وَ إِنْ خِفْتُمْ أَلَّا تُقْسِطُوا فِي الْيَتٰمٰى فَانْكِحُوا مَا طَابَ لَكُمْ
مِّنَ النِّسَآءِ مَثْنٰى وَثُلٰثَ وَرُبٰعَ ۚ فَإِنْ خِفْتُمْ أَلَّا تَعْدِلُوا فَوَاحِدَةً
أَوْ مَا مَلَكَتْ أَيْمَانُكُمْ ۗ ذٰلِكَ أَدْنٰى أَلَّا تَعُوْلُوا 50

وَآتُوا النِّسَآءَ صَدُقٰتِهِنَّ نِحْلَةً 51

That is, forbidden to you are your mothers, and your daughters, and your sisters, and your fathers' sisters, and your mothers' sisters, and the daughters of your brothers, and the daughters of your sisters, and your foster-mothers and your foster-sisters, and the mothers of your wives and your step-daughters

---

47. And furnish yourselves with *necessary* provisions, and surely, the best provision is righteousness. (The Holy Quran, al-Baqarah 2:198)

48. And if you be unclean, purify yourselves by *bathing*. (The Holy Quran, al-Mā'idah 5:7)

49. And in their wealth was a share for one who asked for help and *for* one who could not. (The Holy Quran, adh-Dhāriyāt 51:20)

50. And if you fear that you will not be fair in dealing with the orphans, then marry of women as may be agreeable to you, two, or three, or four; and if you fear you will not deal justly, then *marry only* one or what your right hands possess. That is the nearest *way* for you to avoid injustice. (The Holy Quran, an-Nisā' 4:4)

51. And give the women their dowries willingly. (The Holy Quran, an-Nisā' 4:5)

by your wives with whom you have consorted, but if you have consorted not with them, it shall be no sin upon you, and the wives of your sons, from your loins. You are also forbidden to join two sisters together in marriage; but what has passed has passed.

It is not lawful for you to inherit from women against their will.

It is not lawful for you to marry women whom your fathers had married, except that which happened in the past.

Lawful for you are chaste believing women and chaste women from among those who were given the Book before you, when you give them their dowers, contracting valid marriages, not committing fornication, nor taking secret paramours. In the time of ignorance some of the Arabs who were childless permitted their wives to consort with someone else for the purpose of having a child. The Holy Quran forbade this practice. The expression taking secret paramours has reference to this practice. Then it is said: Destroy not yourselves; and slay not your progeny. Do not enter houses, other than your own, freely like barbarians, until you have obtained leave, and when you have obtained leave and enter, greet the inmates with the salutation of peace. If you find no one therein, then enter not until leave is given to you. If you are told by the inmates to go back then go back.

Do not enter houses by scaling over their walls; enter them through the doors.

When you are greeted with a salutation greet with a better salutation.

Liquor, gambling, idols and divining arrows are but abominations and Satanic devices. So turn wholly away from each one of them.

Forbidden to you is the flesh of a dead animal, and blood, and the flesh of swine; and that on which the name of someone other than Allah is invoked and the flesh of an animal that has been strangled or is beaten to death or is killed by a fall, or is gored to death, and of which a wild animal has eaten and that which has been slaughtered at an altar, for they are all carrion. If they ask thee what is lawful for them, tell them: All good things are lawful for you. Refrain from that which is carrion or resembles carrion or is unclean.

When you are asked to make room for others in your assemblies then hasten to make room so that others might be seated; and when you are asked to rise up, then rise up without delay. Eat of all that is lawful and wholesome like meat, vegetables and pulses etc. but do not be immoderate in any respect. Do not talk at random and talk to the point.

Keep your raiment clean and your bodies and your streets and the places where you sit. Take frequent baths and cultivate the habit of keeping your homes neat and tidy.

Moderate your voice and speak not with a loud voice nor whisper and, except when needed otherwise, walk at a moderate pace, neither too fast nor too slow.

When you go on a journey, make all preparation and take necessary provisions so as to avoid having to beg. When you consort with your spouses, purify yourselves by bathing.

When you eat give out of your food to him who asks and also to dogs and other animals and birds.

There is no harm in your marrying orphan girls who are under your care, but if you apprehend that you may not be fair in dealing with them because they are orphans, then marry women who have parents and relations to be watchful of them, who would respect you and concerning whom you would be careful. You may marry two or three or four of them provided you can deal equitably with all of them. But if you feel that you may not deal justly between them then marry only one, even if you should feel the need of more than one. The limit of four is imposed lest you should be inclined towards marrying a larger number amounting to hundreds according to your old custom and so that you should not incline towards illicit indulgence. Hand over to your wives their dowers freely.

This is the first reform of the Holy Quran whereby man is raised from his natural state and barbaric ways to the status of a civilized social being. In these teachings there is no mention of the higher moral qualities. They are concerned only with elementary human behaviour. This teaching was needed because the people for whose reform the Holy Prophet, peace and blessings of Allah be upon him, was sent, were in an extreme state of barbarity and it was necessary that they should be taught the elementary rules of social behaviour.

Why is the Flesh of Swine Prohibited

One matter to be kept in mind in this context is that in the very name of this animal, God has indicated the reason for the prohibition of its flesh. The Arabic word for swine is *Khinzīr* which is a compound of *Khanz* and *Arā*, which means: I see it very foul. Thus the very name that God Almighty gave to this animal at the beginning points to its uncleanness. It is a curious coincidence that in Hindi this animal is called *Sū'ar*, which is a compound of *Sū'* and *Arā*. This also means: I see it very foul. It should not be a matter of surprise that the Arabic word *Sū'* should have found its way into Hindi. We have established in our book *Minanur-Raḥmān*, that Arabic is the mother of all languages and that many Arabic words are to be found in all languages. Thus *Sū'* is an Arabic word and its equivalent in Hindi is *bad*. This animal is also called *bad* in Hindi. There is no doubt that at the time when Arabic was the universal language this animal was known in this country by an Arabic name which was synonymous with *Khinzīr*, and so it has continued to this day. It is possible that in Sanskrit this word might have undergone some transformation, but the true word is *Khinzīr* which proclaims its own meaning. It is not necessary to enter into a detailed exposition of the foulness of this animal. Everyone knows that it eats filth and is utterly shameless. Thus the reason for the prohibition of its flesh is obvious, as by the law of nature its flesh would have a foul effect on the body and the soul of one who eats it. As we have already demonstrated food affects a person's soul and there can be no doubt that the flesh of such a foul animal would also be foul. Even in pre-Islamic times, Greek physicians had opined that the flesh of this animal particularly damages the faculty of modesty and fosters shamelessness. The eating of carrion is also prohibited in Islamic law for the same reason; that is to say, it affects the moral qualities adversely and is also harmful to physical health. The blood of an animal that is strangled or is beaten to death remains inside the body of the dead animal and they are all carrion. It is obvious that the blood of such an animal is soon corrupted and corrupts the whole flesh. It is established by recent research that the germs in such blood spread a poisonous corruption in the flesh of the dead animal.

Moral Condition of Man

The second part of Quranic reform is that it regulates the natural conditions in such manner as to convert them into high moral qualities. This is a vast subject. If we were to set it forth in detail this paper would become so lengthy that not one tenth of it could be read out in the allotted time. We must, therefore, confine ourselves to the exposition of a few moral qualities by way of illustration.

Moral qualities fall under two heads. First, those moral qualities that enable a person to discard evil; and, secondly, those moral qualities that enable him to do good. Discarding evil comprehends those qualities through which a person tries that he should do no harm to the property, honour or life of a fellow being by his tongue or his hand or his eyes or by any other organ, nor should he design to do him such harm. The doing of good comprehends all those moral qualities whereby a person tries to benefit a fellow being in respect of his property or honour by his tongue or his hand or his knowledge, or by any other means, or determines to make manifest his glory or honour, or overlooks a wrong that had been done to himself and thus benefits the perpetrator of the wrong by sparing him physical pain or financial imposition, or inflicts such chastisement upon him in respect of the wrong which is in reality a mercy for the wrongdoer.

Moral Qualities Related to the Discarding of Evil

The moral qualities that the true Creator has appointed for the discarding of evil are known by four names in Arabic which has a specific name for all human concepts, behaviours and morals.

The first of these moral qualities is called *Iḥṣān*, that is to say, *chastity*. This expression connotes the virtue that is related to the faculty of procreation of men and women. Those men and women would be called chaste who refrain altogether from illicit sex and all approaches to it, the consequence of which is disgrace and humiliation for both parties in this world, and chastisement in the hereafter, and dishonour and grave harm for those related to them. For instance, if a person is guilty of an approach towards the wife of another which, though it does not proceed as far as adultery, yet amounts to its preliminaries, it would become incumbent upon the self-respecting husband of the woman to divorce her on account of her willingness to tolerate such an approach. Her children would also be sadly afflicted. The husband would have to endure all this injury on account of the misconduct of a villain.

It should be remembered that the moral quality of chastity would come into play when a person who possesses the capacity for the compassing of this particular vice restrains himself from indulging in it. If he does not possess that capacity, because he is a minor or is impotent or is a eunuch or has arrived at extreme old age, we cannot give him credit for the moral quality of chastity. He has a natural condition of chastity but, as we have repeatedly pointed out, natural conditions cannot be described as moral qualities. They become moral qualities when they are exercised or become capable of being exercised on their proper occasions, under the control of reason. Therefore, minors and impotent ones and those who deprive themselves in some way of sexual capacity cannot be given credit for this moral quality, though apparently they would be leading chaste lives. In all such cases their chastity would only be a natural condition. As this vice and its preliminaries can be practised by both men and women, the Holy Book of God sets forth directions for both men and women in this context. It says:

قُلْ لِّلْمُؤْمِنِيْنَ يَغُضُّوْا مِنْ اَبْصَارِهِمْ وَ يَحْفَظُوْا فُرُوْجَهُمْ ذٰلِكَ
اَزْكٰى لَهُمْ ...... وَقُلْ لِّلْمُؤْمِنٰتِ يَغْضُضْنَ مِنْ اَبْصَارِهِنَّ وَيَحْفَظْنَ
فُرُوْجَهُنَّ وَلَا يُبْدِيْنَ زِيْنَتَهُنَّ اِلَّا مَا ظَهَرَ مِنْهَا وَلْيَضْرِبْنَ
بِخُمُرِهِنَّ عَلٰى جُيُوْبِهِنَّ ...... وَلَا يَضْرِبْنَ بِاَرْجُلِهِنَّ لِيُعْلَمَ
مَا يُخْفِيْنَ مِنْ زِيْنَتِهِنَّ وَ تُوْبُوْٓا اِلَى اللّٰهِ جَمِيْعًا اَيُّهَ الْمُؤْمِنُوْنَ
لَعَلَّكُمْ تُفْلِحُوْنَ ۝ [52]

وَلَا تَقْرَبُوا الزِّنٰٓى اِنَّهٗ كَانَ فَاحِشَةً وَسَآءَ سَبِيْلًا [53]

وَلْيَسْتَعْفِفِ الَّذِيْنَ لَا يَجِدُوْنَ نِكَاحًا [54]

---

52. Say to the believing men that they restrain their eyes and guard their private parts. That is purer for them..... And say to the believing women that they restrain their eyes and guard their private parts, and that they disclose not their *natural* and *artificial* beauty except that which is apparent thereof, and that they draw their head-coverings over their bosoms,......And they strike not their feet so that what they hide of their ornaments may become known. And turn you to Allāh all together, O believers, that you may succeed. (The Holy Quran, an-Nūr 24:31-32)

53. And come not near unto adultery; surely, it is a foul thing and an evil way. (The Holy Quran, Banī Isrā'īl 17:33)

54. And those who find no *means* of marriage should keep themselves chaste, (The Holy Quran, an-Nūr 24:34)

وَ رَهۡبَانِيَّةَ ۨابۡتَدَعُوۡهَا مَا كَتَبۡنٰهَا عَلَيۡهِمۡ ...... فَمَا رَعَوۡهَا حَقَّ رِعَايَتِهَا ۚ[55]

That is, direct the believing men to restrain their eyes from looking at women outside the prohibited degrees so openly as to be sexually excited by them, and to cultivate the habit of guarding their looks. And should safeguard their private parts at all cost. Likewise they should restrain their ears outside the prohibited degrees that is they should not listen to the singing or beguiling voices of women outside the prohibited degrees nor should they listen to descriptions of their beauty. This is a good way of preserving the purity of their looks and hearts. In the same way, direct believing women that they should restrain their eyes from looking at men outside the prohibited degrees and should safeguard their ears against listening to the voices of such men. That is they should not listen to the voices which sexually excite them. They should cover up their beauty and should not disclose it to anyone outside the prohibited degrees. They should draw their head-coverings across their bosoms and should thus cover up their heads and ears and temples. They should not strike their feet on the

55. But monasticism which they invented for themselves—We did not prescribe it for them......but they did not observe it with due observance. (The Holy Quran, al-Ḥadīd 57:28)

ground like dancers. These are directions following which one can safeguard against moral stumbling.

The second method is to turn to God Almighty and to supplicate Him to be safeguarded against stumbling and slipping. Another direction is: Approach not adultery. This means that one should avoid all occasions that might incite one's mind in that direction, and should eschew all the paths that might lead to this vice. He who indulges in this vice carries his viciousness to the extreme. The way of adultery is an evil way as it obstructs one's progress towards the goal and is extremely harmful to the achievement of the purpose of life. Those who find no means of marriage should keep themselves chaste through the adoption of other means; for instance, through fasting or dieting or exercise.

People sometimes adopt celibacy or submit to castration and take up monasticism. God has not prescribed monasticism and that is why those who adopt it, prove unable to conform to its discipline. This is an indication that if celibacy and monasticism had been imposed by the Divine, everyone would have had to adopt this discipline, in which case the human race would have come to an end long ago. Also, if chastity had to be preserved through castration or any other such device, it would amount to criticism of the Divine Who has bestowed this capacity upon man. Besides, merit depends upon restraining the exercise of a capacity on an improper occasion, through fear of God, and thus acquiring double benefit through its proper exercise. By destroying the capacity a person would deprive himself of both benefits. Merit depends upon the possession of the capacity and its proper regulation. What merit would a person acquire who has lost that capacity and has become like a child? Does a child deserve merit because of his chastity?

Five Remedies Against Unchastity

In these verses God Almighty has not only set forth excellent teaching for acquiring the quality of chastity but has furnished man with five remedies against unchastity. These are: to restrain one's eyes from gazing on those who are outside the prohibited degrees; to restrain one's ears from listening to their voices and to descriptions of their good looks; to avoid occasions which might furnish incitement towards this vice; and to control oneself during the period of celibacy through fasting, dieting etc.

We can confidently claim that this excellent teaching with all its devices that is set forth in the

Holy Quran is peculiar to Islam. It should be kept in mind that as the natural condition of man, which is the source of his passions, is such that he cannot depart from it without a complete change in himself, his passions are bound to be roused, or in other words put in peril, when they are confronted with the occasion and opportunity for indulging in this vice. Therefore, God Almighty has not instructed us that we might freely gaze at women outside the prohibited degrees and might contemplate their beauty and observe all their movements in dancing etc. but that we should do so with pure looks. Nor have we been instructed to listen to the singing of these women and to lend ear to tales of their beauty, but that we should do so with a pure intent. We have been positively commanded not to look at their beauty, whether with pure intent or otherwise, nor to listen to their musical voices or to descriptions of their good looks, whether with pure intent or otherwise. We have been directed to eschew all this as we eschew carrion, so that we should not stumble. It is almost certain that our free glances would cause us to stumble sometime or the other. As God Almighty desires that our eyes and our hearts and all our limbs and organs should continue in a state of purity, He has furnished us with this excellent teaching. There can be no doubt that unrestrained looks become a source of danger. If we place soft bread before a hungry dog, it would be vain to hope that the dog should pay no attention to it. Thus God Almighty desired that human faculties should not be provided with any occasion for secret functioning and should not be confronted with anything that might incite dangerous tendencies.

This is the philosophy that underlies the Islamic regulations relating to the observance of the veil. The Book of God does not aim at keeping women in seclusion like prisoners. This is the concept of those who are not acquainted with the correct pattern of Islamic ways. The purpose of these regulations is to restrain men and women from letting their eyes to rove freely and from displaying their good looks and beauties, for therein lies the good both of men and of women. It should be remembered that to restrain one's looks and to direct them only towards observing that which is permissible is described in Arabic by the expression *ghaḍḍ-e-baṣar*, which is the expression employed in the Holy Quran in this context. It does not behove a pious person who desires to keep his heart pure that he should lift his eyes freely in every direction like an animal. It is necessary that such a one should cultivate the habit of *ghaḍḍ-e-baṣar* in his social life. This is a blessed habit through which his natural impulses would be converted into a high moral quality without interfering with his social needs. This is the quality which is called chastity in Islam.

The **second** quality in the context of the discarding of evil is the one known as *honesty* or *integrity*, that is to say, intolerance of the causing of harm to a fellow being by taking possession of his property dishonestly or unlawfully. Integrity is one of the natural conditions of man. That is why an infant, who follows his natural bent and who has not yet acquired any bad habit, so much dislikes anything belonging to another that it can only be persuaded with difficulty to be suckled by a wet nurse. If a wet nurse is not appointed for it while it is quite small and has not yet developed a keen consciousness, it becomes very difficult for a wet nurse to suckle it. It is naturally disinclined to be suckled by a woman other than its mother. This disinclination sometimes imposes great suffering upon it, and in extreme cases pushes it to the brink of death. What is the secret of this disinclination? It is that it naturally dislikes to leave its mother and to turn to something that belongs to another. When we reflect deeply upon this habit of an infant it becomes clear that this habit is at the root of all honesty and integrity. No one can be credited with the quality of integrity unless his heart becomes charged with dislike and hatred of the property of another as is the case with an infant. But an infant does not always employ this habit on its proper occasion and consequently imposes great suffering upon itself. This habit is only a natural condition which it exhibits involuntarily; it is not, therefore, a moral quality, though it is at the root of the moral quality of integrity. As an infant cannot be described as religious minded and trustworthy because of this habit, so also a person who does not exercise this natural habit on its proper occasion cannot be held to possess this moral quality. It is very difficult to become trustworthy and a person of integrity. Unless a person observes all aspects of integrity he cannot be judged truly trustworthy or honest. In this context God Almighty has instructed us in different aspects of integrity in the following verses:

وَلَا تُؤْتُوا السُّفَهَآءَ اَمْوَالَكُمُ الَّتِيْ جَعَلَ اللّٰهُ لَكُمْ قِيٰمًا وَّارْزُقُوْهُمْ
فِيْهَا وَاكْسُوْهُمْ وَقُوْلُوْا لَهُمْ قَوْلًا مَّعْرُوْفًا ۝ وَابْتَلُوا الْيَتٰمٰى حَتّٰٓى
اِذَا بَلَغُوا النِّكَاحَ ۚ فَاِنْ اٰنَسْتُمْ مِّنْهُمْ رُشْدًا فَادْفَعُوْٓا اِلَيْهِمْ اَمْوَالَهُمْ ۚ
وَلَا تَاْكُلُوْهَآ اِسْرَافًا وَّبِدَارًا اَنْ يَّكْبَرُوْا ؕ وَمَنْ كَانَ غَنِيًّا

فَلْيَسْتَعْفِفْ ۚ وَمَنْ كَانَ فَقِيرًا فَلْيَأْكُلْ بِالْمَعْرُوفِ ۚ فَإِذَا دَفَعْتُمْ
اِلَيْهِمْ اَمْوَالَهُمْ فَاَشْهِدُوْا عَلَيْهِمْ ۚ وَكَفَى بِاللّٰهِ حَسِيْبًا ۝ ٥٦
وَلْيَخْشَ الَّذِيْنَ لَوْ تَرَكُوْا مِنْ خَلْفِهِمْ ذُرِّيَّةً ضِعَافًا خَافُوْا عَلَيْهِمْ ۖ
فَلْيَتَّقُوا اللّٰهَ وَلْيَقُوْلُوْا قَوْلًا سَدِيْدًا ۝ اِنَّ الَّذِيْنَ يَأْكُلُوْنَ اَمْوَالَ
الْيَتٰمٰى ظُلْمًا اِنَّمَا يَأْكُلُوْنَ فِيْ بُطُوْنِهِمْ نَارًا ۚ وَسَيَصْلَوْنَ سَعِيْرًا ۝ ٥٧

That is, should there be among you a person of property who is an orphan or minor and it is apprehended that he would waste his property through his lack of sense, you should take charge of his property as a custodian and should not hand it over to him, inasmuch as the whole system of commerce and social security depends upon proper care of property. Out of the income of the property you should provide for the maintenance of its owner

---

56. And give not to the foolish your property which Allāh has made for you a means of support; but feed them therewith and clothe them and speak to them words of kind advice. And prove the orphans until they attain the *age* of marriage; then, if you find in them sound judgment, deliver to them their property; and devour it not in extravagance and haste against their growing up. And whoso is rich, let him abstain; and whoso is poor, let him eat *thereof* with equity. And when you deliver to them their property, then call witnesses in their presence. And Allāh is sufficient as a Reckoner. (The Holy Quran, an-Nisā' 4:6-7)

57. And let those fear *God* who, if they should leave behind them their own weak offspring, would be anxious for them. Let them, therefore, fear Allāh and let them say the right word. Surely, they who devour the property of orphans unjustly, only swallow fire into their bellies, and they shall burn in a blazing fire. (The Holy Quran, an-Nisā' 4:10-11)

and you should instruct him in all equitable values that would help to develop his reason and understanding and would furnish him with proper training so that he should not remain ignorant and inexperienced. If he is the son of a merchant he may be instructed in the ways of business and commerce, and if his father followed some profession or other occupation he may be given training in some appropriate occupation. Test him from time to time whether he is making progress in his training. When he arrives at the age of maturity, that is to say about 18 years, and you perceive that he has developed enough intelligence to look after his property, hand over his property to him. Do not deal with his property wastefully while it is in your charge, out of the apprehension that when he grows up he will take it over from you. If the custodian is in easy circumstances he should not make any charge for administering the property. But if he is poor, let him make use of as much of it as is fair.

The custom among Arab custodians of an orphan's property was that the property was used as capital for commerce and out of its profit provision was made for the orphan and thus the capital was not destroyed. The custodian made a fair charge for looking after the property. This is the system to which reference is made in these verses. Then it is said: When you hand over the property to its owner you should do so before witnesses.

Those of you who are likely to leave behind minor children should give no directions by way of testament which should operate unfairly against the children. Those who consume the substance of orphans unjustly only devour fire into their bellies and shall enter a blazing fire.

It is to be observed how many aspects of honesty and integrity God Almighty has set forth in these verses. A truly honest person is one who keeps in mind all these aspects. If this is not done with perfect intelligence his trustworthiness would cover many hidden dishonesties.

Then it is directed:

وَلَا تَاْكُلُوْٓا اَمْوَالَكُمْ بَيْنَكُمْ بِالْبَاطِلِ وَتُدْلُوْا بِهَآ اِلَى الْحُكَّامِ لِتَاْكُلُوْا
فَرِيْقًا مِّنْ اَمْوَالِ النَّاسِ بِالْاِثْمِ وَاَنْتُمْ تَعْلَمُوْنَ ○ [58]

اِنَّ اللّٰهَ يَاْمُرُكُمْ اَنْ تُؤَدُّوا الْاَمٰنٰتِ اِلٰٓى اَهْلِهَا [59]

اِنَّ اللّٰهَ لَا يُحِبُّ الْخَآئِنِيْنَ [60]

---

58. And do not devour your wealth among yourselves through falsehood, and offer it not *as bribe* to the authorities that you may knowingly devour a part of the wealth of other people with injustice. (The Holy Quran, al-Baqarah 2:189)

59. Verily, Allāh commands you to make over the trusts to those entitled to them, (The Holy Quran, an-Nisā' 4:59)

60. Surely, Allāh loves not the treacherous. (The Holy Quran, al-Anfāl 8:59)

وَاَوْفُوا الْكَيْلَ اِذَا كِلْتُمْ وَزِنُوْا بِالْقِسْطَاسِ الْمُسْتَقِيْمِ ۭ 61

وَلَا تَبْخَسُوا النَّاسَ اَشْيَآءَهُمْ وَلَا تَعْثَوْا فِي الْاَرْضِ مُفْسِدِيْنَ 62

وَلَا تَتَبَدَّلُوا الْخَبِيْثَ بِالطَّيِّبِ ۠ 63

Do not devour each other's substance through deceit and falsehood, nor offer your wealth as a bribe to the authorities, that you may deliberately acquire a part of other people's wealth through injustice. Make over the trusts to those entitled to them. Allah does not love those who are dishonest.

Give full measure when you measure out, and weigh out with a true balance. Do not deliver short, and do not go about creating disorder in the land. This means that you should not go about in the land with an evil intent, to commit theft or robbery or to pick pockets or to acquire the property of other people through unlawful means. Then he said: do not give that which is defective in exchange for that which is good; that is to say, as embezzlement is unlawful, so the sale of defective articles representing them as being in good

61. And give full measure when you measure, and weigh with a right balance; (The Holy Quran, Banī Isrā'īl 17:36)

62. 'And diminish not unto people their things, nor act corruptly in the earth, making mischief. (The Holy Quran, ash-Shu'arā' 26:184)

63. And give to the orphans their property……and devour not their property with your own. Surely, it is a great sin. (The Holy Quran, an-Nisā' 4:3)

condition, and the exchange of defective articles in return for good ones, is also unlawful.

In all these verses God Almighty has set forth all dishonest practices in such a comprehensive way that no type of dishonesty has been omitted. He has not merely forbidden theft, lest a stupid person should consider that though theft is forbidden all other improper methods of acquiring property are permitted. Forbidding all improper methods of acquiring property in a comprehensive way is true wisdom. In short, if a person does not possess the quality of integrity in all its aspects, he would not be considered honest even if he exhibits honesty in certain matters. That would be only his natural condition, shorn of reasonable discrimination and true insight.

The **third** moral quality in the context of discarding evil is designated in Arabic as *hudnah* or *haun*, which means refraining from inflicting physical pain on anyone and behaving peacefully. Without a doubt, peacefulness is a high moral quality and is essential for humanity. The natural impulse corresponding to this moral quality, the regulation of which converts it into a moral quality, which is possessed by an infant, is attachment. It is obvious that in his natural condition man is unable to conceive of peacefulness or combativeness. In that condition the impulse of attachment that he exhibits is the root of peacefulness, but as it is not exercised under the control of reason or reflection and with deliberation, it is not accounted a moral quality. It becomes a moral quality when a person deliberately makes himself harmless and exercises the quality of peacefulness on its proper occasion, and refrains from using it out of place. In this context the Divine teaching is:

وَاَصْلِحُوْا ذَاتَ بَيْنِكُمْ [64]

وَالصُّلْحُ خَيْرٌ ط [65]

وَاِنْ جَنَحُوْا لِلسَّلْمِ فَاجْنَحْ لَهَا [66]

وَعِبَادُ الرَّحْمٰنِ الَّذِيْنَ يَمْشُوْنَ عَلَى الْاَرْضِ هَوْنًا [67]

وَاِذَا مَرُّوْا بِاللَّغْوِ مَرُّوْا كِرَامًا [68]

اِدْفَعْ بِالَّتِيْ هِيَ اَحْسَنُ فَاِذَا الَّذِيْ بَيْنَكَ وَبَيْنَهٗ عَدَاوَةٌ كَاَنَّهٗ
وَلِيٌّ حَمِيْمٌ [69]

---

64. And set things right among yourselves, (The Holy Quran, al-Anfāl 8:2)

65. And reconciliation is best. (The Holy Quran, an-Nisā' 4:129)

66. And if they incline towards peace, incline you also towards it, (The Holy Quran, al-Anfāl 8:62)

67. And the servants of the Gracious *God* are those who walk on the earth in a dignified manner, (The Holy Quran, al-Furqān 25:64)

68. And when they pass by anything vain, they pass on with dignity; (The Holy Quran, al-Furqān 25:73)

69. Repel *evil* with that which is best. And lo, he between whom and yourself was enmity will become as though he were a warm friend. (The Holy Quran, Ḥā Mīm as-Sajdah 41:35)

جَزٰٓؤُا سَيِّئَةٍ سَيِّئَةٌ مِّثْلُهَا ۚ فَمَنْ عَفَا وَاَصْلَحَ فَاَجْرُهٗ عَلَى اللّٰهِ [75]

That is, good men are those who control their empers when they are roused and who overlook people's faults when that is appropriate. The ecompense of an injury is a penalty in proportion hereto; but whoso forgives and effects thereby a reform n the offender, and no harm is apprehended, that is to say, exercises forgiveness on its appropriate occasion, will have his reward with Allah.

This verse shows that the Quran does not teach non-resistance to evil on all occasions, or that nischief makers and wrongdoers should never be punished. Its teaching is that one must consider whether the occasion calls for forgiveness or punishment, and to adopt the course which would be best in the interests both of the offender and the public. Sometimes an offender turns away from wrongdoing in consequence of being forgiven, and sometimes forgiveness incites him to further wrongdoing. Therefore, God Almighty directs that we should not develop the habit of forgiving blindly on all occasions, but should consider carefully whether forgiveness or punishment would be most

5. And the recompense of an injury is an injury the like thereof; but whoso forgives and *his act* brings about reformation, his reward is with Allāh. (The Holy Quran, ash-Shūrā 42:41)

That is, try to promote accord between yourselves; Peace is best; when they incline towards peace, do you incline towards it also. The true servants of the Gracious One walk upon the earth in humility; and when they come upon something vain, which might develop into strife, they pass on with dignity, that is to say, they do not start quarrelling over trifles and do not make small matters which do not cause much harm an occasion for discord. The expression "vain" that is employed in this verse means mischievous utterance of words or doing something which causes little damage and does little harm. Peacefulness means that one should overlook conduct of that type and should act with dignity; but if a person's conduct does real harm to life or property or honour, the moral quality that should come into play in apposition to it is not peacefulness but forbearance, to which we shall revert later. Should anyone behave mischievously towards you, you should try to repel it with peacefulness, whereby he who is your enemy will become your warm friend. In short, peacefulness means overlooking trivial matters of annoyance which occasion no great harm, and are more or less confined to uttering nonsense.

The **fourth** moral quality in the context of discarding evil is courtesy or a good word. The natural impulse which is at the root of this moral quality is cheerfulness. Before an infant is able to express itself in words, it displays cheerfulness as a substitute for courtesy and good talk. That shows that the root of courtesy is cheerfulness which is a natural faculty and is converted into the moral quality of courtesy by being used on its proper occasion. The Divine teaching in this context is:

وَقُوْلُوْا لِلنَّاسِ حُسْنًا [70]

لَا يَسْخَرْ قَوْمٌ مِّنْ قَوْمٍ عَسٰۤى اَنْ يَّكُوْنُوْا خَيْرًا مِّنْهُمْ وَلَا نِسَآءٌ
مِّنْ نِّسَآءٍ عَسٰۤى اَنْ يَّكُنَّ خَيْرًا مِّنْهُنَّ ۚ وَلَا تَلْمِزُوْۤا اَنْفُسَكُمْ
وَلَا تَنَابَزُوْا بِالْاَلْقَابِ ؕ [71]

اجْتَنِبُوْا كَثِيْرًا مِّنَ الظَّنِّ ۫ اِنَّ بَعْضَ الظَّنِّ اِثْمٌ وَّلَا تَجَسَّسُوْا وَ
لَا يَغْتَبْ بَّعْضُكُمْ بَعْضًا ؕ ...... وَاتَّقُوا اللّٰهَ ؕ اِنَّ اللّٰهَ تَوَّابٌ رَّحِيْمٌ [72]

وَلَا تَقْفُ مَا لَيْسَ لَكَ بِهٖ عِلْمٌ ؕ اِنَّ السَّمْعَ وَالْبَصَرَ وَالْفُؤَادَ
كُلُّ اُولٰٓئِكَ كَانَ عَنْهُ مَسْـُٔوْلًا [73]

70. And speak to men kindly (The Holy Quran, al-Baqarah 2:84)

71. Let not one people deride *another* people, who may be better than they, nor let women *deride other* women, who may be better than they. And defame not your own people, nor call one another by nicknames. (The Holy Quran, al-Ḥujurāt 49:12)

72. Avoid most of suspicions; for suspicion in some cases is a sin. And spy not, nor back-bite one another......And fear Allāh, surely, Allāh is Oft-Returning *with compassion* and is Merciful. (The Holy Quran, al-Ḥujurāt 49:13)

73. And follow not that of which you have no knowledge. Verily, the ear and the eye and the heart—all these shall be called to account. (The Holy Quran, Banī Isrā'īl 17:37)

That is, say to people that which is goo
one people deride another people, haply tl
better than themselves; nor let one group
deride another, haply the last may be b
the first. Defame not your people nor
names. Eschew too much suspicion; Als
nor backbite one another. Do not char
with anything of which you have no p
remember that the ear and the eye and
will all be called to account.

Moral Qualities Related to the of Good

The second type of moral qualities are
are related to doing good. The first o
forbearance or forgiveness. He who co
offence against another causes him pain o
deserves to be punished either through the
the law, with imprisonment or fine, or dire
person offended. To forgive him, if f
should be appropriate, would be to do hin
this context the teaching of the Holy Qur

كٰظِمِيْنَ الْغَيْظَ وَالْعَافِيْنَ عَنِ النَّاسِ ؕ [74]

74. And those who suppress anger and pardon men; (The H
'Imrān 3:135)

appropriate, and, therefore, a virtue, in each particular case, and should adopt that course. Some people are so vindictive that they keep in mind the wrongs done to their fathers through generations, and there are others who carry forbearance and forgiveness to the extreme, sometimes even to the limit of shamelessness. They exercise such weakness, forgiveness and forbearance as are utterly inconsistent with dignity, honour, and chastity. Their conduct is a stain on good character and the result of their forgiveness and forbearance is that people are disgusted with them. That is why the Holy Quran attaches the condition of appropriate time and place for the exercise of every moral quality, and does not approve the exercise of a moral quality out of its place.

It should be remembered that forgiveness is not a moral quality in itself. It is a natural impulse which is found in children also. A child soon forgets an injury, if it is inflicted upon him wrongfully, and again approaches affectionately the person who has inflicted the injury upon him, even if such a person should intend to kill him. He is pleased with his beguiling words. Such forgiveness is in no sense a moral quality. It would become a moral quality when it is exercised in its proper place and on its proper occasion; otherwise it would only be a natural impulse. There are few people who are able to distinguish between a natural impulse and a moral quality. We have repeatedly pointed out the distinction between a true moral quality and a natural condition, which is that a moral quality is conditioned by conformity to place and occasion, and a natural impulse often comes into play out of place. A cow is harmless and a goat is humble but we do not attribute these qualities to them because they are not invested with a sense of time and place. Divine wisdom and God's true and perfect Book have made every moral quality subject to time and place for its proper exercise.

The second moral quality in this category is equity, and the third is benevolence and the fourth is graciousness as between kindred. God, the Glorious, has said:

إِنَّ اللَّهَ يَأْمُرُ بِالْعَدْلِ وَالْإِحْسَانِ وَإِيتَاءِ ذِي الْقُرْبَىٰ وَيَنْهَىٰ عَنِ الْفَحْشَاءِ وَالْمُنْكَرِ وَالْبَغْيِ ۚ [76]

This means that we are commanded to return good for good, and to exercise benevolence when it is called for, and to do good with natural eagerness as

76. Verily, Allāh enjoins justice, and the doing of good to others; and giving like kindred; and forbids indecency, and manifest evil, and wrongful transgression. (The Holy Quran, an-Naḥl 16:91)

between kindred, when that should be appropriate. God Almighty forbids transgression or that you should exercise benevolence out of place or should refrain from exercising it when it is called for; or that you should fall short of exercising graciousness as between kindred on its proper occasion, or should extend it beyond its appropriate limit. This verse sets forth three gradations of doing good.

The **first** is the doing of good in return for good. This is the lowest gradation and even an average person can easily acquire this gradation that he should do good to those who do good to him.

The **second** gradation is a little more difficult than the first, and that is to take the initiative in doing good out of pure benevolence. This is the middle grade. Most people act benevolently towards the poor, but there is a hidden deficiency in benevolence, that the person exercising benevolence is conscious of it and desires gratitude or prayer in return for his benevolence. If on any occasion the other person should turn against him, he considers him ungrateful. On occasion he reminds him of his benevolence or puts some heavy burden upon him. The benevolent ones have been admonished by God Almighty:

لَا تُبۡطِلُوۡا صَدَقٰتِكُمۡ بِالۡمَنِّ وَالۡاَذٰى[77]

That is, O those who do good to others–good that should be based on sincerity–do not render it vain by reminding them what favours you have done them or by inflicting injury on them. The Arabic word for alms (*Ṣadaqah*) is derived from a root (*ṣidq*) that means sincerity. If the heart is not inspired by sincerity in bestowing alms, the almsgiving ceases to be alms and becomes mere display. That is why those who exercise benevolence have been admonished by God Almighty not to render vain their benevolence by reproaches or injury.

The **third** grade of doing good is graciousness as between kindred. God Almighty directs that in this grade there should be no idea of benevolence or any desire for gratitude, but good should be done out of such eager sympathy as, for instance, a mother does good to her child. This is the highest grade of doing good which cannot be exceeded. But God Almighty has conditioned all these grades of doing good with their appropriate time and place. The verse cited above clearly indicates that if these virtues are not exercised in their proper places they would become vices. For instance, if equity exceeds its limits it

77. Render not vain your alms by taunt or injury. (The Holy Quran, al-Baqarah 2:265)

would take on an unwholesome aspect and would become indecent. In the same way, misuse of benevolence would take on a form which would be repelled by reason and conscience; and in the same way graciousness between kindred would become transgression. The Arabic word for transgression is *baghī*, which connotes excessive rain which ruins crops. A deficiency in the discharge of an obligation or an excess in its discharge are both *baghī*. In short, whichever of these three qualities is exercised out of place becomes tainted. That is why they are all three qualities conditioned by the due observance of place and occasion. It should be remembered that equity or benevolence or graciousness between kindred are not in themselves moral qualities. They are man's natural conditions and faculties that are exhibited even by children before they develop their reason. Reason is a condition of the exercise of a moral quality and there is also a condition that every moral quality should be exercised in its proper place and on its proper occasion.

There are several other directions set out in the Holy Quran concerning benevolence which are all made subject to the condition of place and time.

It is said:

يٰۤاَيُّهَا الَّذِيْنَ اٰمَنُوْۤا اَنْفِقُوْا مِنْ طَيِّبٰتِ مَا كَسَبْتُمْ ...... وَلَا تَيَمَّمُوا
الْخَبِيْثَ مِنْهُ [78]

لَا تُبْطِلُوْا صَدَقٰتِكُمْ بِالْمَنِّ وَالْاَذٰى ۙ كَالَّذِيْ يُنْفِقُ مَالَهٗ رِئَآءَ النَّاسِ [79]
وَاَحْسِنُوْا ۚ اِنَّ اللّٰهَ يُحِبُّ الْمُحْسِنِيْنَ [80]

اِنَّ الْاَبْرَارَ يَشْرَبُوْنَ مِنْ كَاْسٍ كَانَ مِزَاجُهَا كَافُوْرًا ۝ عَيْنًا يَّشْرَبُ
بِهَا عِبَادُ اللّٰهِ يُفَجِّرُوْنَهَا تَفْجِيْرًا ۝ [81]

وَيُطْعِمُوْنَ الطَّعَامَ عَلٰى حُبِّهٖ مِسْكِيْنًا وَّيَتِيْمًا وَّاَسِيْرًا ۝ اِنَّمَا
نُطْعِمُكُمْ لِوَجْهِ اللّٰهِ لَا نُرِيْدُ مِنْكُمْ جَزَآءً وَّلَا شُكُوْرًا ۝ [82]

وَاٰتَى الْمَالَ عَلٰى حُبِّهٖ ذَوِي الْقُرْبٰى وَالْيَتٰمٰى وَالْمَسٰكِيْنَ وَابْنَ
السَّبِيْلِ ۙ وَالسَّآئِلِيْنَ وَفِي الرِّقَابِ ۚ [83]

---

78. O you who believe! spend of the good things that you have earned,......and seek not what is bad to spend out of it (The Holy Quran, al-Baqarah 2:268)

79. Render not vain your alms by taunt and injury, like him who spends his wealth to be seen of men, (The Holy Quran, al-Baqarah 2:265)

80. And do good; surely, Allāh loves those who do good. (The Holy Quran, al-Baqarah 2:196)

81. But the virtuous drink of a cup, tempered with camphor—A spring wherefrom the servants of Allāh drink. They make it gush forth—a forceful gushing forth. (The Holy Quran, ad-Dahr 76:6-7)

82. And they feed, for love of Him, the poor, the orphan, and the prisoner, *Saying*, 'We feed you for Allāh's pleasure *only*. We desire no reward nor thanks from you. (The Holy Quran, ad-Dahr 76:9-10)

83. And spends his money for love of Him, on the kindred and the orphans and the needy and the wayfarer and those who ask *for charity*, and for *ransoming* the captives; (The Holy Quran, al-Baqarah 2:178)

إِذَآ أَنْفَقُوْا لَمْ يُسْرِفُوْا وَلَمْ يَقْتُرُوْا وَكَانَ بَيْنَ ذٰلِكَ قَوَامًا 84

وَالَّذِيْنَ يَصِلُوْنَ مَآ أَمَرَ اللّٰهُ بِهٖٓ أَنْ يُّوْصَلَ وَيَخْشَوْنَ رَبَّهُمْ
وَيَخَافُوْنَ سُوْٓءَ الْحِسَابِ 85

وَفِيْٓ أَمْوَالِهِمْ حَقٌّ لِّلسَّآئِلِ وَالْمَحْرُوْمِ 86

الَّذِيْنَ يُنْفِقُوْنَ فِي السَّرَّآءِ وَالضَّرَّآءِ 87

وَأَنْفَقُوْا مِمَّا رَزَقْنٰهُمْ سِرًّا وَّعَلَانِيَةً 88

إِنَّمَا الصَّدَقٰتُ لِلْفُقَرَآءِ وَالْمَسٰكِيْنِ وَالْعٰمِلِيْنَ عَلَيْهَا وَالْمُؤَلَّفَةِ
قُلُوْبُهُمْ وَفِي الرِّقَابِ وَالْغٰرِمِيْنَ وَفِيْ سَبِيْلِ اللّٰهِ وَابْنِ السَّبِيْلِ
فَرِيْضَةً مِّنَ اللّٰهِ وَاللّٰهُ عَلِيْمٌ حَكِيْمٌ 89

لَنْ تَنَالُوا الْبِرَّ حَتّٰى تُنْفِقُوْا مِمَّا تُحِبُّوْنَ 90

---

84. When they spend, are neither extravagant nor niggardly but moderate between the two; (The Holy Quran, al-Furqān 25:68)

85. And those who join what Allāh has commanded to be joined, and fear their Lord, and dread the evil reckoning; (The Holy Quran, ar-Ra'd 13:22)

86. And in their wealth was a share for one who asked for help and *for* one who could not. (The Holy Quran, adh-Dhāriyāt 51:20)

87. Those who spend in prosperity and adversity, (The Holy Quran, āl-e-'Imrān 3:135)

88. And spend out of that with which We have provided them, secretly and openly, (The Holy Quran, ar-Ra'd 13:23)

89. The alms are only for the poor and the needy, and for those employed in connection therewith, and for those whose hearts are to be reconciled, and for the *freeing of* slaves, and for those in debt, and for the cause of Allāh, and for the wayfarer—an ordinance from Allāh. And Allāh is All-Knowing, Wise. (The Holy Quran, at-Taubah 9:60)

90. Never shall you attain to righteousness unless you spend out of that which you love; (The Holy Quran, āl-e-'Imrān 3:93)

وَاٰتِ ذَا الۡقُرۡبٰى حَقَّهٗ وَالۡمِسۡكِيۡنَ وَابۡنَ السَّبِيۡلِ وَلَا تُبَذِّرۡ تَبۡذِيۡرًا [91]

وَّبِالۡوَالِدَيۡنِ اِحۡسَانًا وَّبِذِى الۡقُرۡبٰى وَالۡيَتٰمٰى وَالۡمَسٰكِيۡنِ وَالۡجَارِ ذِى
الۡقُرۡبٰى وَالۡجَارِ الۡجُنُبِ وَالصَّاحِبِ بِالۡجَنۡۢبِ وَابۡنِ السَّبِيۡلِ ۙ وَمَا
مَلَكَتۡ اَيۡمَانُكُمۡ ؕ اِنَّ اللّٰهَ لَا يُحِبُّ مَنۡ كَانَ مُخۡتَالًا فَخُوۡرَا ۙ الَّذِيۡنَ
يَبۡخَلُوۡنَ وَيَاۡمُرُوۡنَ النَّاسَ بِالۡبُخۡلِ وَيَكۡتُمُوۡنَ مَاۤ اٰتٰٮهُمُ اللّٰهُ مِنۡ
فَضۡلِهٖ ؕ [92]

That is, O ye who believe, spend by way of generosity or benevolence or charity such of your wealth as you have acquired lawfully, that is to say, no part of which has been acquired through theft or bribery or dishonesty or embezzlement or wrongdoing. Do not select for charity out of it that which is useless or unclean.

Render not vain your alms with reproaches or injury, that is to say, never remind your donee that you had bestowed anything on him nor inflict any injury upon him, for in such case your charity would

---

91. And give you to the kinsman his due, and to the poor and the wayfarer, and squander not *your wealth* extravagantly. (The Holy Quran, Banī Isrā'īl 17:27)

92. And *show* kindness to parents, and to kindred, and orphans, and the needy, and to the neighbour that is a kinsman and the neighbour that is a stranger, and the companion by *your* side, and the wayfarer, and those whom your right hands possess. Surely, Allāh loves not the proud *and* the boastful. Who are niggardly and enjoin people to be niggardly, and conceal that which Allāh has given them of His bounty. (The Holy Quran, an-Nisā' 4:37-38)

be rendered vain, nor spend your money merely for display. Be benevolent towards your fellow beings, for Allah loves those who are benevolent.

The truly virtuous shall drink of a cup tempered with camphor. The reference to camphor means that their hearts will be cleansed of all the burning desires and impure urges of the world. The root of the Arabic word for camphor connotes suppression, or covering up, which means that their illicit emotions will be suppressed and they will become pure hearted and will enjoy the coolness of understanding. Then it is said that they will drink from a spring which they shall cause to gush forth from the earth through their efforts. This indicates a deep mystery of the philosophy of paradise. Let him who has understanding understand it.

Then he said: the truly virtuous feed the poor, the orphan, and the captive for the love of Allah with such foods as they eat themselves, assuring them: We are not laying you under any obligation but feed you only to win Allah's pleasure. We desire no return or thanks from you. This is an indication that they exercise the third grade of doing good which proceeds out of pure sympathy.

The truly virtuous are in the habit of spending their wealth out of love of God on their kindred and on the upbringing and training of orphans and in making provision for the poor and for providing comfort for travellers and for those who ask and for procuring the freedom of slaves and discharging the burdens of those who are in debt.

They are neither extravagant nor niggardly, but keep a balance between the two. They join together that which Allah has bidden to be joined, and fear their Lord. In their wealth those who ask and those who are unable to ask have a right. By those who are unable to ask are meant animals such as dogs, cats, sparrows, oxen, donkeys, goats and others that cannot express their needs in words.

They do not hold back in times of scarcity or famine, but continue to spend at such times also according to their capacity. They spend in charity secretly and openly; secretly, so that they might safeguard themselves against displaying their charity, and openly, so that they might set an example for others. That which is set aside for charity should be spent on the poor and the needy, and on those employed in connection with its collection and distribution, and to help those who have to be rescued from some evil, and on procuring the freedom of slaves, and on those burdened with debts, and the afflicted and on other purposes which are purely for the sake of God and on those striving in the cause of Allah.

You cannot attain the highest grade of virtue unless you spend for the promotion of the welfare of your fellow beings that part of your wealth which you hold dear.

Render to the poor their due and to the needy and the wayfarer but safeguard yourselves against extravagance. This is a direction to restrain people from spending unnecessarily on weddings and luxuries and on the occasion of the birth of a child etc.

Be benevolent towards parents and kindred, and orphans and the needy and the neighbour who is a kinsman, and the neighbour who is not related to you, and the wayfarer and your servants and your horses and your cattle and your other animals that you possess. This is what God loves. He loves not those who are heedless and selfish, and those who are niggardly and enjoin other people to be niggardly, and conceal their wealth and tell those who are needy that they have nothing which they can give them.

True Courage

Of the natural conditions of man is that which resembles courage, as an infant sometimes seeks to time when the wrongdoers were bent on the ruin of the righteous. In these circumstances, if Islam had not had recourse to measures of self defence, thousands of innocent women and children would have been slaughtered and an end would have been put to Islam.

It is a great error on the part of our opponents that they imagine that revealed guidance must under no circumstances inculcate resistance to the enemy and should always demonstrate its love and mercy by way of meekness and gentleness. Such people imagine that they display great reverence for God, the Lord of Honour and Glory, by attributing to Him only the qualities of gentleness and tenderness. But those who are given to reflection and pondering can easily perceive that such people are involved in gross and obvious error. A contemplation of the Divine law of nature clearly shows that it certainly is pure mercy. But that mercy does not manifest itself by way of gentleness and tenderness in all circumstances. Out of pure mercy, like an expert physician, it sometimes administers a sweet draught to us and at other times it prescribes a bitter medicine for us. Divine mercy deals with us as each of us deals mercifully with his body. There can be no doubt that each of us loves his whole body and if anyone wishes to pull out a single hair of ours we are much annoyed with him. Yet despite the fact that the love that we bear towards our body is distributed over the whole of it, and all our limbs are dear to us, and we do not desire the loss or hurt any of them, it is clear that our love for every one of our limbs is not of the same degree and quality. In fact, the love of our principal limbs upon which largely depends the carrying out of our purposes, prevails over our hearts. Similarly in our estimation the totality of our limbs is far greater than our love for any particular limb. Thus when we are confronted with a situation in which the security of a superior limb depends upon wounding or cutting or breaking an inferior limb, we reconcile ourselves to such an operation. We are grieved at the wounding or cutting of a limb that is dear to us, but through the apprehension lest the disorder of the inferior limb should operate to destroy a superior limb, we are reluctantly reconciled to its cutting. This illustration should help us to realize that when God observes that His righteous servants are in peril of being destroyed at the hands of the worshippers of falsehood and that this would lead to great disorder He manifests His appropriate design, whether from heaven or from earth, for the safeguarding of the righteous and for the putting down of disorder; for as He is رحیم Merciful, He is also حکیم Wise.

اَلْحَمْدُ لِلّٰهِ رَبِّ الْعٰلَمِيْنَ All praise belongs to Allah the Lord of the Universe.

Index

Names and Places

Names

Places